McKITTRICK CANYON

McKITTRICK CANYON

A BEAUTIFUL HISTORY

DONNA BLAKE BIRCHELL

THE History PRESS

Published by The History Press
Charleston, SC 29403
www.historypress.net

First published 2015

Manufactured in the United States

ISBN 978.1.62619.868.5

Library of Congress Control Number: 2014957557

For my mother, Dorothy Hodge Blake, whose inner and outer beauty rivaled anything seen in these pages and who even attracted the attention of angels. You are missed every day.

Those who contemplate the beauty of the earth find reserves of strength that will endure as long as life lasts.
—Rachel Carson

The tendency nowadays to wander in wildernesses is delightful to see. Thousands of tired, nerve-shaken, over-civilized people are beginning to find out that going to the mountains is going home; that wilderness is a necessity; and that mountain parks and reservations are useful not only as fountains of timber and irrigating rivers, but as fountains of life.
—John Muir

CONTENTS

ACKNOWLEDGEMENTS

I want to extend a special thank-you to my late parents, William and Dorothy Blake, who first introduced me to McKittrick Canyon as a child and told me many stories, including how they drove their 1952 Buick into the canyon to visit with resident Wallace Pratt. Thank you for showing me your favorite spot on earth.

Thank you once again to technical librarian extraordinaire and great friend Samantha Villa, who was the catalyst behind this entire journey. As always, you're the best!

A huge thank-you to senior acquisitions editor Christen Thompson, whose guidance through this journey was done with professionalism and grace. It was great working with you on this project—you're the best!

The entire staff of The History Press, you are wonderful! Special thank you to Will Collicott and Danielle Raub for all of your extra special efforts on my behalf. Really appreciate you!

To Robert House, former Guadalupe Mountains National Park interpretive ranger, and Robert Hoff, former park historian, I will be forever indebted to you both for your dedication to and research on the Guadalupe Mountains National Park, including McKittrick Canyon. Thank you for doing such an awesome job preserving history!

Thanks to the staff of the Guadalupe Mountains National Park and Carlsbad Caverns National Park for preserving McKittrick Canyon and the entire GUMO system for future generations—you should be highly commended!

Superintendent Dennis Vasquez, Michael Hainey, Elizabeth Fields and Karl Pierce have provided courtesy and information above and beyond. Without these fine public servants and keepers of history, this book would not have seen the light of day. Thank you also for being excited about this project!

An extra special thank-you to Dr. Jonena Hearst for taking customer service to a new level and for stepping in to help a bewildered author organize images and navigate the Guadalupe Mountains National Park archives.

Many thanks to librarians Sybil Walterscheid and Julie Danielson Pearson at the Carlsbad Public Library for all your diligence in locating books and interlibrary loans. I couldn't have done it without your help!

To all the researchers and historians who forged the trail before me, my hat is off to you, and my heartfelt appreciation goes to you as well.

A special thank-you to former school librarian and super-woman volunteer Carol Belski, who was instrumental in getting me on the right track. I appreciate your expert advice.

To the staff and volunteers of the Living Desert Zoo & Gardens State Park and Gift Shop, thank you for your constant support and friendship throughout the writing of this book and the others—it meant the world to me!

Words cannot express the gratitude I have for my wonderful and patient family, who endured this experience without complaint and with pride. You are my rock, my strength, Jerry, Michael and Justin Birchell. I send you much love and thank you all from the bottom of my heart. You make all of this worthwhile!

INTRODUCTION

Known for its great diversity, McKittrick Canyon has long been a subject of study for geologists, who have described the Guadalupe Mountains as "an island in the sky." The Capitan Reef, of which McKittrick Canyon is carved, is over 250 million years old and provides a natural laboratory for scientists all over the world to examine.

The Most Beautiful Spot in Texas

Long declared "the most beautiful spot in Texas" by a founding landowner, Wallace E. Pratt, and many others, McKittrick Canyon certainly lives up to its moniker, especially during the fall season. The canyon is a place of distinctive and rare beauty, rivaling the eastern seaboard with its spectacular array of brilliant colors. Many hikers find it hard to fathom that such scenic splendor can reside in an arid Texas desert landscape.

The life source for the canyon is McKittrick Canyon Creek, whose two main branches provide water for the wildlife, vegetation and aquatic life in the canyon. This creek is now home to descendants of rainbow trout that were introduced into the waters in the 1930s by county judge of Culberson County, Texas, and rancher Jesse C. Hunter Sr. These rainbow trout make up the only self-sustaining trout population in Texas.

Evidence of ancient man is scattered throughout the canyon but not seen by the everyday tourist/hiker. Rock art and mescal pits are still visible and provide anthropologists and archaeologists with a glimpse into the obscure, ancient history of McKittrick Canyon. The Guadalupe Mountain range played a huge role in the lives of the native people who roamed in the deep canyons.

A pristine environment, McKittrick Canyon is preserved by the National Park Service, which made an agreement with the first landowners, who sold their acreage to the park for as little as twenty-two dollars per acre, to keep the canyon as untouched parkland for as long as possible. The long history of McKittrick Canyon, the park, began many years before there was even a road to access the area. By 1931, there were two highways connecting Carlsbad, New Mexico, with El Paso, Texas, approximately 178 miles away.

Biologist and bird conservationist J. Stokely Ligon, author of *New Mexico Birds: Where to Find Them*, and many others noted after attending a large overnight picnic hosted by Judge Hunter's corporation, Grisham-Hunter, in McKittrick Canyon that the canyon should be opened to the public. He envisioned a scenic loop road that would commence at the White Sands National Monument, close to Alamogordo, New Mexico, and encompass El Paso, Texas; El Capitan of the Guadalupe Mountains; and Roswell, New Mexico. However, Ligon was adamant that no roads should be built in the canyons themselves, allowing access only to the mouth. He noted, "The great trouble with us is that an ease-loving people want to sit in their cars and reach the few spots of natural wild life and then the wild life vanishes." Ligon loved the Guadalupes enough to build a ranch home near Nickel Creek, which is within eyeshot of El Capitan.

GIFT OF NATURE

McKittrick Canyon is a true hidden jewel, a gift of nature and an adventure not to be missed. As part of the vast Chihuahuan Desert, McKittrick Canyon is home to a complex mixture of vegetation and native wildlife, creating a natural classroom that attracts many teams of scientists from all spectrums of the scientific community to the unique region.

The canyon is a beloved destination for the thousands who come every year to enjoy the gifts nature has to offer, especially in late October to early November, when the foliage turns brilliant shades of red, orange, yellow and brown. The sheer white limestone walls of McKittrick Canyon against a typically azure blue sky create the perfect backdrop for some of the most beautiful photographs you will ever take.

The National Park Service is extremely proud of the Guadalupe Mountains National Park and would like to relay to the public the necessity to follow all rules and obey all signs in the park, which are there not only for your safety but also to protect the park for future generations who will come behind you to enjoy the spectacular vistas you have already enjoyed.

Young artist and poet Clark Alonzo Cox traveled on foot to the Guadalupe Mountains National Park and was one of the first Anglos to climb to the top of Guadalupe Peak and dub it the "Top o' Texas." Cox was so taken by the beauty of McKittrick Canyon that he wrote the following tribute:

McKittrick Canyon, land of dreams
Majestic in your virgin wild,
With every turn new beauty teems
Love, primitive and undefiled.
Love to scale your rugged sides
Or climb the deer trails o'er the steep
Or dunk where cooling water glides
Within your bosom dark and deep.
Or scan the cliffs for hidden lair
And watch the antics of the fox
Or playing cubs and mother bear
High up among the cave cleft rocks.
Or lie and watch the drifting clouds
Low o'er the outline of the height
Now reaching down like fleecy shrouds
To hide the topmost peaks from sight.
The maples in their autumn dress
From yellow tints to flaming red
Transform the slopes from soberness
Into a mammoth flower bed.
Farewell, McKittrick, land of dreams
Your towering crag and wooded slopes
Your sylvan dell and running streams
Will bring me back again I hope.

As you hike along the rocky floor of McKittrick Canyon, stop to take a deep, long breath of the crisp high desert air and forget the hustle and bustle of the world you left behind to reflect on the diversity of your surroundings and those who stood there before you thousands of years ago. Rugged mountains, tiny wildflowers, chirping birds, a mule deer peeking out from behind a piñon tree, the distant sound of wind rushing through the ponderosa pine boughs and the bubbling of the pristine creek will take you to a simpler time when the earth was still young.

Although the canyon has seen many tremulous years with twists and turns, the final result far outshines any trouble felt along the way.

DIVERSITY

McKittrick Canyon is a hidden beauty, full of history and awe-inspiring views. Native Americans, settlers, scientists and government officials alike have known the great value of this rare attraction and, luckily for the rest of us, have all sought to preserve this unique canyon for future generations.

In all beautiful things, diversity is a huge factor. Out of the ordinary and a bubble off plumb, McKittrick Canyon is one of the most diverse spots on earth. It is known as a place for all seasons—each equally spectacular. The cheerful arrays of wildflowers that dot the landscape in spring give way to the lush green grasses produced by the monsoonal rains in summer. Fall is when McKittrick shines and nature shows off its artistic talents, but winter, in its stark silence, brings a whole new perspective as Jack Frost paints the foliage in ice.

No matter which season you choose to visit McKittrick Canyon, you will undoubtedly be amazed by the sights that await you on your journey. It is almost guaranteed you will stop many times during your trek to simply drink in the amazing beauty that surrounds you. The contrast between desert and forest, arid and lush and starkness and sheer splendor will astonish you throughout the entire hike. Hopefully, you will develop a passion for this rare gem of a canyon and tell everyone you know so that they can experience it for themselves.

It is my hope that when you read this book, you will come away with a new understanding of what a priceless piece of this wonderful planet is contained within the limestone walls of McKittrick Canyon. It is a fragile ecosystem that must be preserved for future generations.

CHAPTER 1
THE EVOLUTION OF MCKITTRICK CANYON

One can only imagine the sheer force and energy it took to form the Permian Barrier Reef, also known as the Capitan Reef, through volcanic eruptions and earthquakes as the earth's complexion began to form over 250 million years ago. This was a violent time of great upheaval, landslides and seismic activity—a time when earth was becoming the collection of landscapes we are all familiar with today. Acknowledged by geologists the world over, the Guadalupe Mountains have received the distinct honor of being included in the Geological Time Scale and of being referred to as the Guadalupian Global Stratotype.

Contrary to their name, the Guadalupe Mountains are not actual mountains—they are remnants of the Permian Reef Complex. Some of the first indications of fossils were written about in 1855 by geologist Dr. G.G. Shumard (who now has a peak named in his honor), who was exploring the mountains in search of artesian water wells. His writings were not studied until 1920, however, when the oil industry became interested in the area as well. It was then that E.R. Lloyd, K.H. Crandall, W.G. Blanchard and M.J. Davis were sent to the region to investigate and develop the reef hypothesis that stands today.

The two-thousand-foot Guadalupian Lamar limestone palisades that line McKittrick Canyon are evidence of a tremendous geologic uplift in the Pliocene and early Pleistocene times resulting from severe tectonic fracturing. Scientists have debated whether the canyon was once a large, enclosed cavern like the Carlsbad Caverns and whether it was actually a part

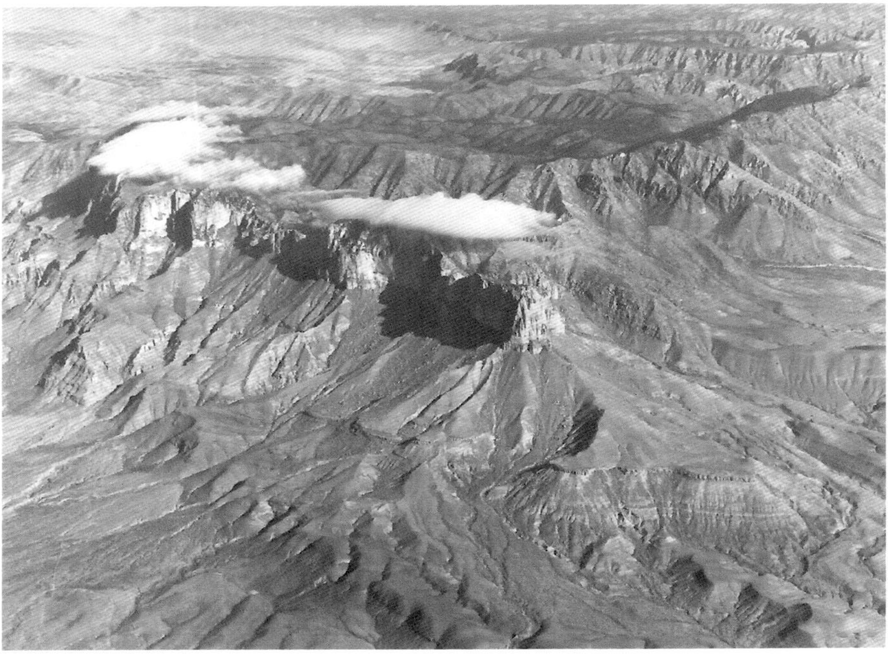

This 1964 aerial view of the Guadalupe Mountains and McKittrick Canyon shows the vastness of the area and the wide-open spaces of the Permian Basin. *Courtesy Guadalupe Mountains National Park.*

of that system at one time. There is evidence of massive boulders consisting of calcium carbonate on the canyon floor that mimic those found in the caves to the north.

McKittrick Canyon and the Capitan Reef grew horizontally more than vertically largely on their own talus, or debris field. The reef is considered to be one of the geologic wonders of the world. The Guadalupe Mountains are a geological horseshoe that divides the Delaware Plain to the south and the Salt Basin to the west. The Capitan Reef, at over 350 miles long and 30 miles wide, is the most expansive formation of its kind ever recorded.

Covered by a shallow ocean called the Permian Sea, the Permian Basin saw the waters recede slowly during the last ice age due to a massive uplift, which prevented the sea from receiving sufficient amounts of water. This, coupled with the arid climate, caused a rapid evaporation, and this process revealed the magnificent limestone formations now present. At one point in time, the water at the base of the reef was 1,500 feet deep.

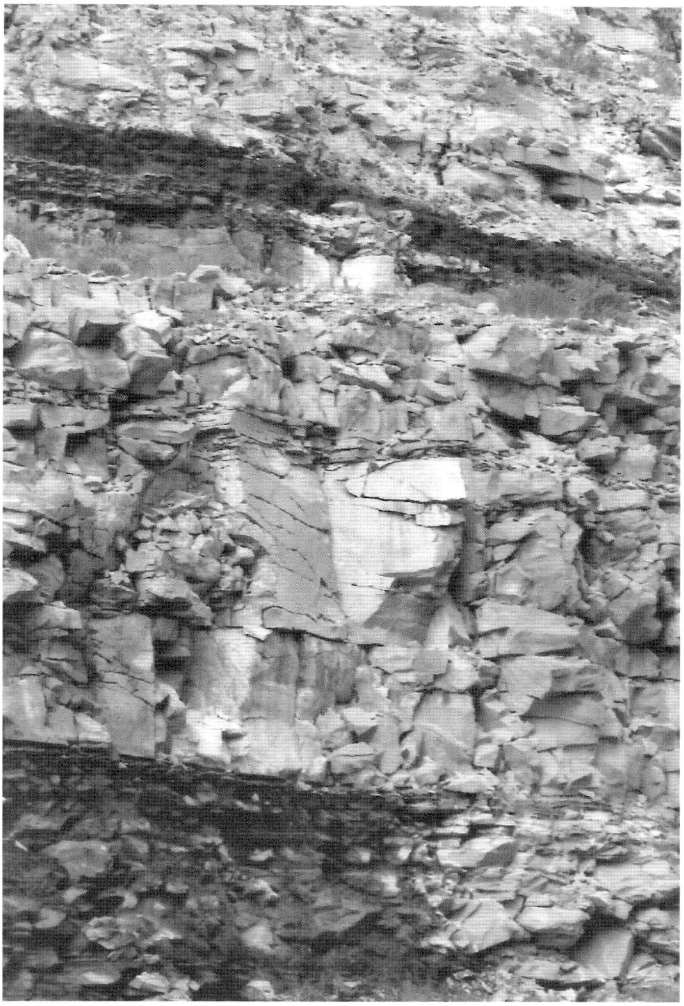

Sediment layers that form the Capitan Reef are highly evident in the exposed road construction cutouts along Highway 62/180 between Carlsbad, New Mexico, and El Paso, Texas. *Author's collection.*

A supercontinent known as Pangea was formed as two large landmasses thundered together to form one during the Permian period. As a result of this period ending, the "worst mass extinction in the history of the Earth" occurred, according to a paper authored by the National Park Service, which reported that nearly 90 percent of species became extinct. The cause of this extinction is still under debate.

As you drive along Highway 62/180 en route to El Paso, Texas, before you get to the McKittrick Canyon turnoff, you will see road construction cutouts on the side of the road that reveal the composite structure of the mountains. These rock faces give clues to the many layers of the fossilized reef, which is composed of back-reef materials, fore-reef materials and reef-building organisms. Some of the prime reef builders were brachiopods, bryozoans and corals, which mixed with sediment to form a concrete-like substance and create the reef structure.

The National Park Service reported that by 1980, over five hundred species of fossils had been found in McKittrick Canyon, which took over 220,000 years to form. Some of the largest fossil remains include those of the giant ground sloth, the mastodon and the saber-toothed tiger.

A geological mecca, McKittrick Canyon has been seen in textbooks used by students the world over. The canyon is also the primary field site for geology students from Texas Tech University in Lubbock. The name of Wallace E. Pratt, an early explorer and the first geologist for Humble Oil, is

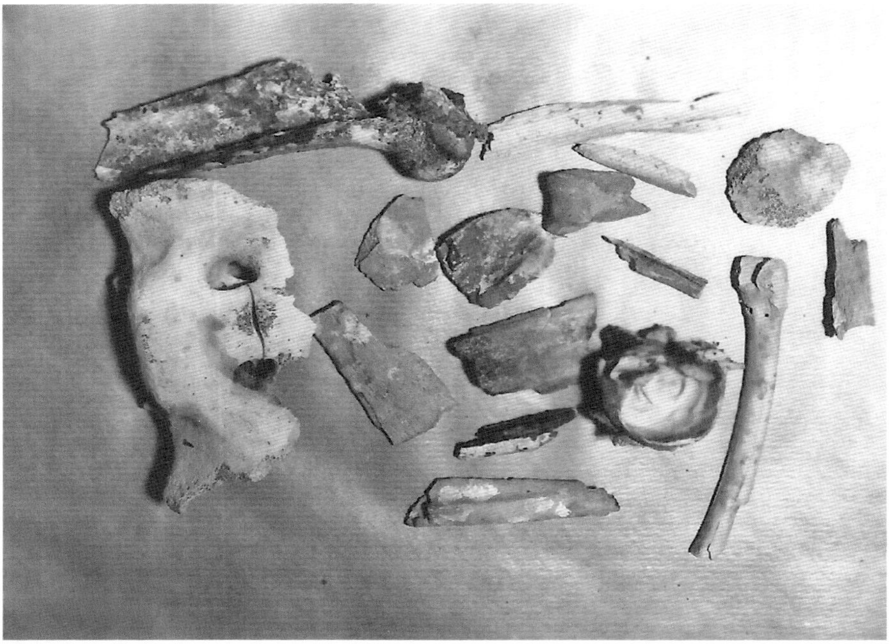

Evidence of ancient life can be found throughout the Guadalupe Mountains National Park, as well as in McKittrick Canyon. Archaeologists have uncovered bones of many extinct species that once resided in the area. Tools left by prehistoric man have also been catalogued. *Courtesy Guadalupe Mountains National Park.*

equally well known among scholars. Pratt was known to have commented, "I want this place to be a place where geologists can come and poke and look around and learn from what's here." Stewardship of this diverse canyon has been passed on to those who have followed in Pratt's shoes—not an easy feat to accomplish.

Travertine deposits have created dams along the free-flowing stream that runs the length of the canyon (which includes nine waterfalls); however,

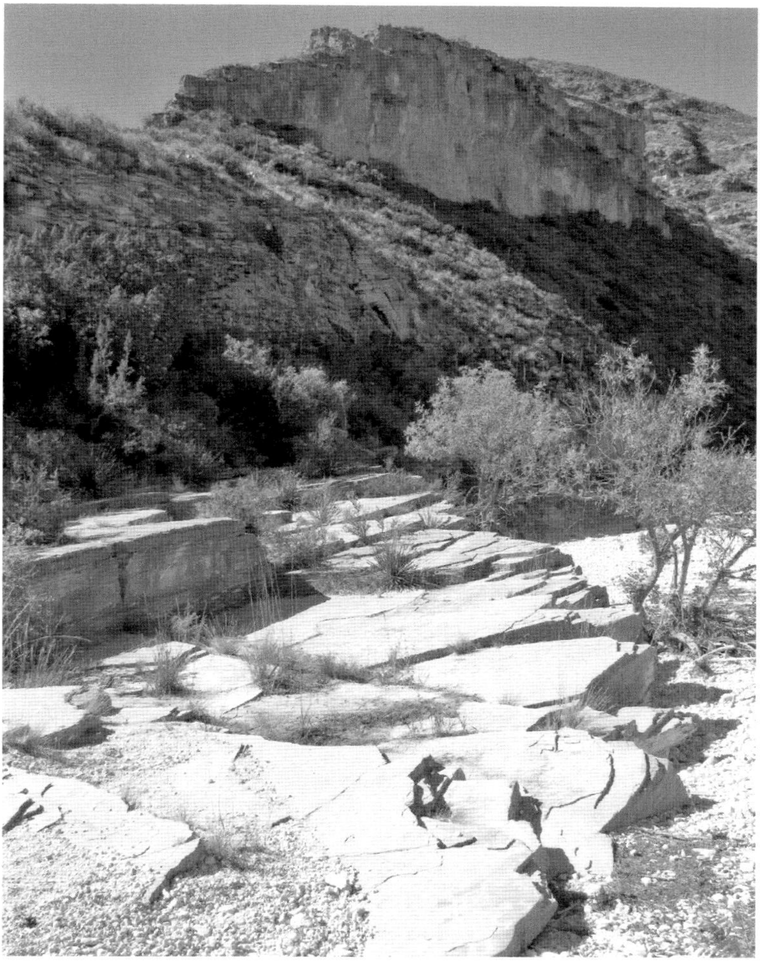

After many years of constant water flow rich in calcium carbonate, the bed of McKittrick Creek was washed smooth, forming layers of fragile travertine. Due to several severe floods (some recent), the travertine dams have been destroyed, leaving gravel and boulders in their wake. *Author's collection.*

most of these dams were destroyed by the floods of 1943 and 1968. By means of natural occurrences such as floods and earthquakes, the flow of this stream has changed many times over its lifetime, sending most of the water underground. McKittrick Canyon Creek has three divisions: North McKittrick Creek, South McKittrick Creek and a lower portion that runs downstream toward the present-day visitors' center.

A reported 5.8-magnitude earthquake hit Valentine, Texas, at 5:04 a.m. on August 16, 1931. The quake was also felt in Culberson County and resulted in numerous rock falls and slides in the foothills of the Guadalupe Mountains near Carlsbad, New Mexico, which is over 150 miles away. In fact, waves were felt as far east as Oklahoma and south as Coahuila, Mexico, for a total of 400,000 square miles. Most of the damage was in Valentine, with crumbling buildings as the result. The headstones in the small town's cemetery were actually rotated during the worst of the quake. This quake affected the points in which the live stream in McKittrick Canyon presented itself; in some cases, areas of water were left dry and vice-versa. It is also responsible for stopping the flow of the spring at Pine Springs. To date, it is the strongest earthquake ever reported in the state of Texas.

It is reported that Texas fault lines are not always vertical, forming oil traps, which were thought to leak. These traps formed the huge oil deposit fields that are being developed today.

Through the urgings of landowner J.C. Hunter Sr. and E.H. Simons, manager of the El Paso, Texas Chamber of Commerce, Texas governor-elect W. Lee O'Daniel toured McKittrick Canyon in 1938 and was so impressed that he "pledged to do everything he could to establish a park there." Unfortunately, it would be many more years before this would come to pass.

As part of the Chihuahuan Desert, which spans 200,000 square miles from the bottom of Mexico to just above Albuquerque, New Mexico, the lower part of McKittrick Canyon is known as a brush desert, consisting of sagebrush, mesquite bushes and drought-resistant foliage.

Longtime Hunter Ranch foreman Noel Kincaid stated in a 1963 *El Paso Times* article, "In McKittrick, the formations are open, whereas they are underground and somewhat transformed in the Carlsbad Caverns."

The cliff located behind the Stone Cabin (Pratt Cabin) in McKittrick Canyon is said to be the only site in North America to have observed the formation of an ocean reef. The famous canyon has been written up in many geology journals and studied widely by members of universities as well as amateur geologists, all of whom have marveled at the diversity that comprises the Capitan Reef structure.

CHAPTER 2

SACRED PLACE FOR NATIVE AMERICANS

The Guadalupe Mountains have always provided shelter, food and a way of life for the native peoples who roamed the area as far back as twelve thousand years ago as hunter-gatherers, a fact attested to by a recovered Folsom point and other artifacts. Because of its opposing size, the mountain range was given many names, and few other than the native tribes explored it.

In the many dry caves scattered across the Guadalupe Mountains, and in McKittrick Canyon specifically, archaeologists have located scraping tools; cordage; tools fashioned from antlers, maños and matates; baskets; sandals; beads; shell fragments; and, of course, human remains from various time periods. Pictographs have also been discovered in the shelters and many caves scattered in the Guadalupe Mountains, as well as in McKittrick Canyon.

Evidence of early life includes bone fragments, charcoal remnants and pottery shards found in the caves and overhangs along the canyon. There are over four hundred recorded archaeological sites in Guadalupe Mountains National Park alone, many dating back to 1000 BC. Rock art, a distinctive feature found in small caves and overhangs all throughout the park, shows scenes of early life and some now-extinct mammals that existed during that period, including the dire wolf and the ground sloth.

Pratt Cave, which is located along the northeastern portion of the south side of McKittrick Canyon, yielded artifacts such as disc beads, water vessels, animal hides, basketry, wooden tools, bear-grass matting, food sources and human remains believed to date back to the Late

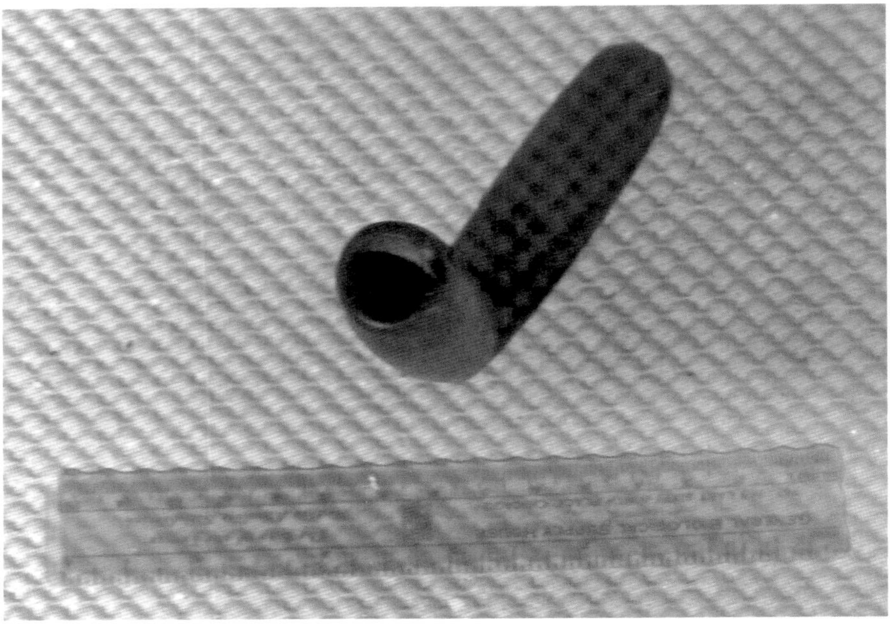

This polished stone pipe, one of two found on the toe slope below a cave at the mouth of McKittrick Canyon, is thought to be from the Upper Archaic period. Specimens such as these have also been found at sites in Buena Vista Park, California. *Courtesy Guadalupe Mountains National Park.*

Archaic (circa AD 540) period. This cave was excavated in 1961 by Albert Schroeder, a government archaeologist, along with National Park Service employees Phil Van Cleve, Lyndon Hargrave, William H. Balgemann and Ranger Roger Reisch. It was determined to be an early Mescalero cave site. Projectile points and midden rings found in South McKittrick Canyon by researchers Susana and Paul Katz also indicate that the site was highly utilized in the Late Archaic era.

It is thought that the early inhabitants of the Guadalupe Mountains were of the Jornada branch of the Mogollon culture. This culture would soon become the Athabaskan family, which came to the area from what are now the eastern slopes of the Canadian Rockies, and the Mescalero Apache, who were called *Querechos* by Spanish explorer Coronado in the 1540s. (It was also thought that the Mescalero tribe was of Sarsi descent in the Athabaskan family.) The tribe was given the name *apachu* by the Spanish explorers who first encountered them during their 1598 *entrada* into the New World, a name that meant "enemy," according to the Zuñi tribe. The name *mescalero*, which

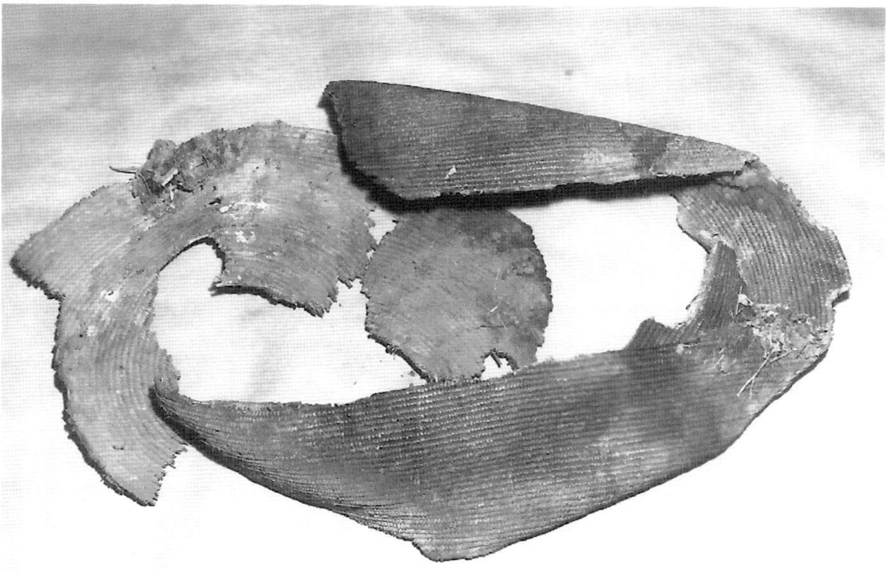

Basket remnants found in a cave at the mouth of McKittrick Canyon have been dated to AD 540. *Courtesy Guadalupe Mountains National Park.*

meant, in extremely loose literal Spaniard terms, "mescal-eating raccoons," was later added and would eventually morph into Mescalero Apache, a name that the Ndé (the name they called themselves) deeply despised. The Spaniards were not complimentary of the Ndé, whose dark complexions accentuated the whites of their eyes and gave them what the Spanish described as a rough exterior appearance.

As a branch of the Lipan Apache, who lived mainly in the Davis Mountains, located nearly two hundred miles away, the Mescalero moved to the Guadalupe Mountains in their search for food. Names given to themselves and by other tribes are far more flattering and include Shis-Inday (People of the Mountain Forests), Nadahéndé (People of the Mescal) and Nitahéndé (People Who Live Against the Mountains). But they would be known as the N'de in present times and overall the Tse' I Chi (pronounced Say-ee-Chee).

The tribe followed the seasons and animals to different regions of the mountains in a circular or sun-wise pattern, always beginning in the east. Since the number four is sacred for the Ndé, most of what they did in their lives revolved around the number: four seasons (spring, summer, fall and winter), four colors (yellow, white, blue and black), four directions (north, east, south

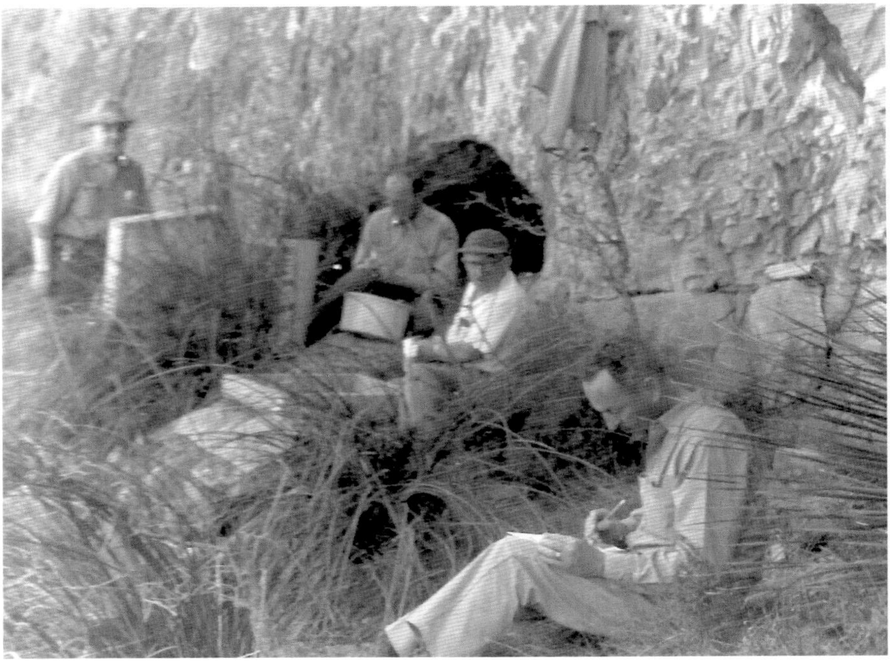

Professional and amateur archaeologists alike worked together to discover the ancient history of McKittrick Canyon. *From left to right*: William Balgemann, P.F. Van Cleave, Lyndon Hargrave and Al Schroeder. *Courtesy Guadalupe Mountains National Park.*

and west), four animals (grizzly bear, eagle, pronghorn and bison) and four spirits (spider, mirage, whirlwind and black obsidian), to name but a few.

Time is also sacred to the Mescalero Apache. As anthropologist Hans Peter Duerr noted, "Sacred time and space is not a specific time or place but a time between times, time filling gaps between different realities. Sacred time is not past, present or future time; it has no 'location' whatever on the continuum of time."

McKittrick Canyon was a beautiful, isolated place that provided abundant sustenance and much-needed protection to the native tribes. Many archaeological sites have been discovered at about every elevation of the canyon. Some of the most visited and well-used sites are located in the high regions.

Originally coming from the northern parts of what is now New Mexico and Colorado, the Mescalero Apache, a nomadic tribe, found the Guadalupe Mountains much to their liking, as the magnificent formations provided the people with most of their needs.

Long rumored to be cursed, the Guadalupe Mountains remained largely uninhabited or explored by other cultures up until the early 1600s, except for the early Spanish during the entrada of 1598. The Spanish entrada in the area with explorer Don Juan Oñate used the Guadalupe Mountains as a resting point before crossing the salt flats and desert en route to El Paso, Texas. The two cultures clashed many times, causing the Spanish to be wary of the mountain range.

It would be the Spanish who would introduce the horse to the New World. The horse, which was extremely important, was seen by the Apache tribes as a gift from the gods because of its many uses. The tribe began the first of many raids to obtain horses from other tribes and settlers in 1630, reaching a peak in 1660.

One of the largest populations of native tribes is the Mescalero Apache, who, according to William "Bill" H. Balgemann, an avid amateur archaeologist who developed many studies on the Guadalupe Mountains, were in the region from AD 1400 to AD 1900. The "Ancient People" groupings written by Balgemann are as follows:

25,000 BC to 15,000 BC—Mid Paleo Indians
15,000 BC to 7,000 BC—Late Paleo Indians
7,000 BC to 3,000 BC—Early Guadalupian Cave Dwelling Basket Makers
3,000 BC to 1,000 BC—Mid Guadalupian Cave Dwelling Basket Makers
1,000 BC to AD 1,400—Late Guadalupian Cave Dwelling Basket Makers
AD 1,400 to AD 1,900—Mescalero and Lipan Apache (nomadic groups)

Constant conflict between the Apache tribes and the Comanche tribes would cause much strife in the region for not only the native people but early settlers and travelers as well.

The Apache lived in leather teepees, brush *jacals* or *wickiups*, grass huts with thatched roofs. These were made with locally available wood such as sotol or ocotillo stalks. Easy to transport from various campsites, the wood is also light since it is generally hollow. Bottoms of the shelters would then be ringed with rocks, called midden rings, which can still be found all over the Guadalupe Mountains region.

It is reported that the Mescalero liked to live on the edge—quite literally. They believe that to be in true harmony with the environment, you must live on the edges of mountains, as anything you pray for is heard on the edge. An early student of the Mescalero Apache culture, Harry W. Basehart, wrote, "The people think the mountain is a holy place…people go to the mountain

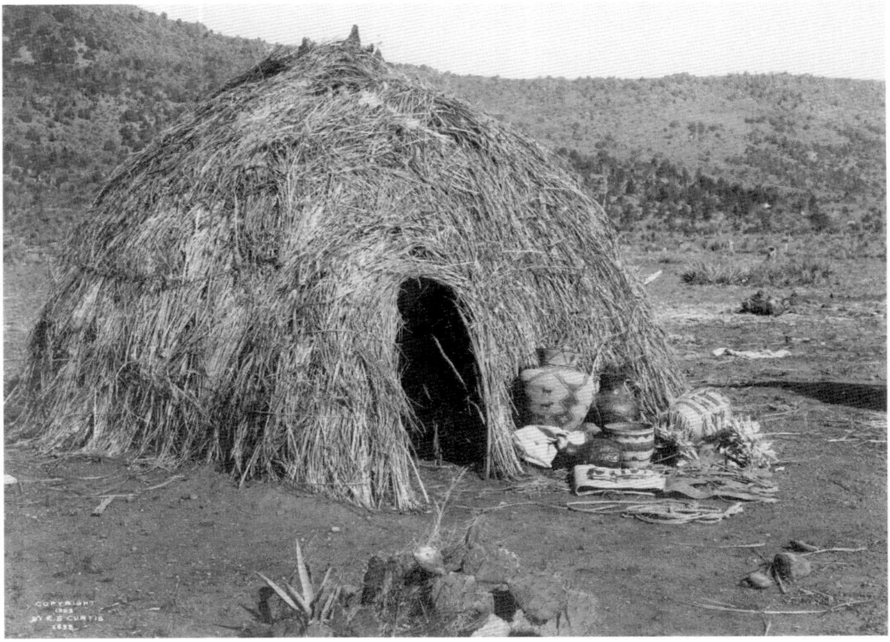

As a nomadic tribe, the Mescalero Apaches lived in teepees made from animal hides supported by wooden poles or, at times, a more substantial structure called a wickiup, which was made from mud, sticks and grasses. *Courtesy Library of Congress.*

and raise their hand up to the mountain and pray for all good things, that no sickness will come to them and that the good luck will be with them. With all of their faith they put into praying while at the mountain so they get their wish."

The Apache feel the plants and animals willingly give their seeds, meat, fruit and hides to them—but only if they (plants and animals) are approached with the appropriate rituals and rules. For example, older tribes believed that the hunters had to hunt on an empty stomach; otherwise, the deer would not show themselves.

Archaeological investigations of the Guadalupe Mountains did not begin in earnest until the 1970s, although some sites were worked and recorded as early as the 1930s. In 1970, with the efforts of Harry J. Shafer of the University of Texas, the Texas Archeological Society became involved, bringing volunteers to the Guadalupe Mountains to conduct surveys on over 150 sites, 139 of which were previously undocumented locations.

The Mescalero were some of the first-known environmentalists in that they were so in tune with the environment. They were taught early on to

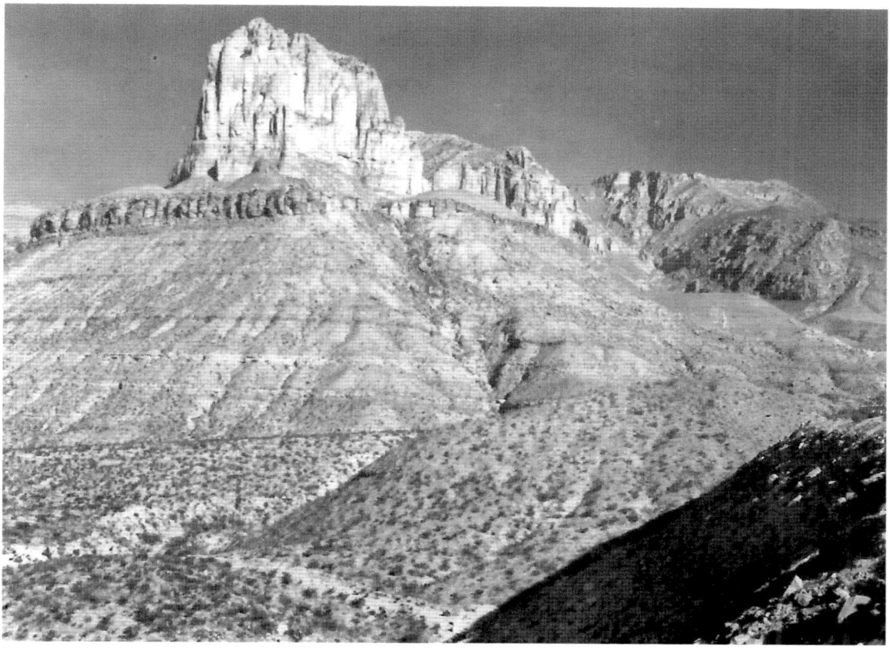

Guadalupe Peak, shown here just behind the famed El Capitan, is considered the most sacred place for the Ndé people. It is at this peak that the Mescalero tribe believes the White Painted Woman began creation. *Author's collection.*

have great respect for the world and nature. Although they were nomadic, they did not leave much behind when they moved on, as everything that was not needed was incinerated before leaving the area.

The Guadalupe Mountains, especially Guadalupe Peak, were home to the Creator Goddess, White Painted Woman, who the Apache believe was the first woman on earth and the mother of all. The Mescalero Apache territory is within a 150-mile radius of the center of the sacred mountain; therefore, the tribe is categorized as "desert people," although they like to refer to themselves as "mountain people."

Mescalero women are the most vital part of the tribe, as they are the caregivers, food gatherers and healers in the society. It was the women who would harvest the mescal (agave) hearts and other chief plants required for the well-being of the tribe. It is their belief that the "Ant People" are responsible for showing the women the mescals that are ripe enough to harvest. Ants are attracted to the sap or juices of the mescal crowns, which is sweet and is said to be a sure sign that the agave is about to bloom.

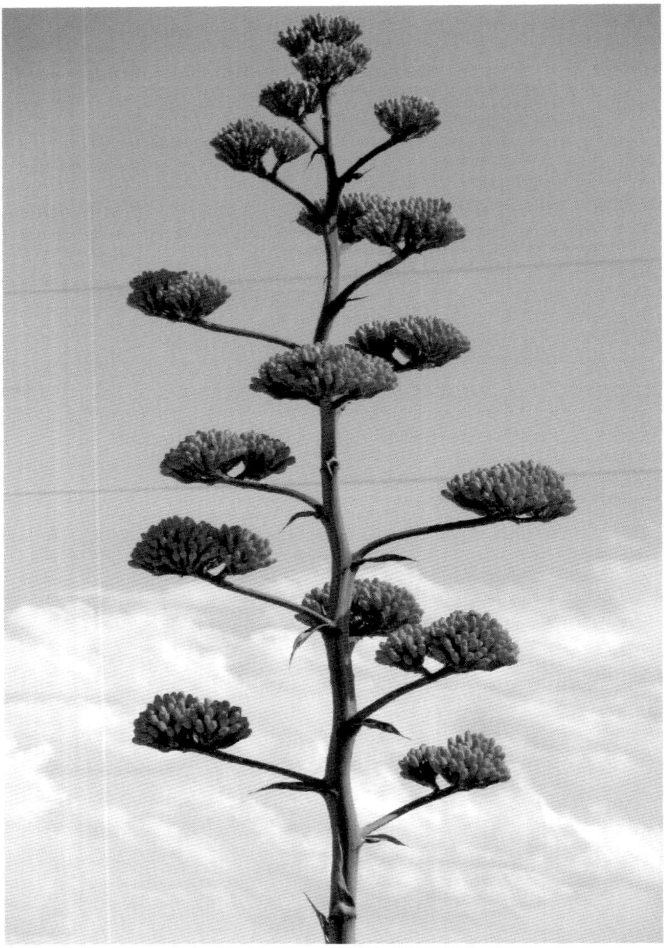

The agave plant, also known as the century plant, provided the main source of sustenance for the early tribes and is the core of the ancestral rituals still celebrated by the modern tribes. *Author's collection.*

The agave (pronounced a-GAV-ay) (*Agave neomexicana*), also known as mescal (pronounced mess-KAHL) or the century plant, grows to heights of almost twenty feet and is the most important food source of the tribe. Contrary to the name, the century plant produces a stalk with bloom about every ten years; sadly, this is also the signal that the plant will not survive after the blooms wilt.

When Captain Randolph B. Marcy of the Fifth Infantry was sent to the Southwest during his famous expedition in 1849, he described a variety of plants that were unusual to the men from back east. One of these plants was the "maguey plant," which was later determined to be the mescal plant.

Being such a vital plant to the Mescalero Apache, the agave is used completely. The seeds are ground into flour, the blooms are boiled and eaten and the fibrous leaves are turned into bowstrings, cradles, mats, ropes, sandals and animal snares. Distilled, the mescal turns into what many of the early settlers described as "liquid hell"—tequila, as it is known today.

Both male and female tribe members wore their hair long, usually adorned with feathers and beads. The typical garb for the women was a buckskin gown with hand-painted native symbols, the outer fringe of which was sometimes decorated with tin triangles, especially on the ceremonial clothes and the fringe bottoms of the mescal gathering baskets. These triangles have been found in and around mescal pits that were used to roast the sacred plant.

In tune with nature, the Mescalero Apache tribe followed the seasons to take full advantage of their offerings. The four most widely used wild plant food sources were mescal, piñon, mesquite and datil. The light rains of spring brought the tender flowers on useful plants such as mesquite bushes, which produce beans that are thought by both the natives and settlers to be the key to a long life. Mesquite bean jelly was a popular item eaten in the Guadalupe Mountains. The Apache were also known to plant roses along their trails. Today, remnants of these plants can still be seen.

In the culture of the Ndé people, many animals were highly prized or completely avoided, according to custom. The bear, which symbolized the supernatural, was given much respect and avoided if possible. Canine species such as coyotes, wolves and foxes also held special powers that were thought could bring harm to the person who took the animal's pelt. The coyote, known as a clever trickster, is the star of many tales told throughout the ages.

Killing of the mountain lion was avoided, if possible, by the native people because the animal was highly revered and considered a friend. It was thought to be bad luck to take the big cat's life even though legend also told that the hunter would then possess the hunting luck of the animal through its death.

The white explorers were not as respectful and described killing a "panther." Texas Ranger John Ford found the animal to be unpalatable, writing in his memoirs, "It had a peculiar fresh taste, very difficult to get rid of."

Other mammals, reptiles and amphibians that were never eaten by the people were snakes, because they were feared; frogs; and porcupines.

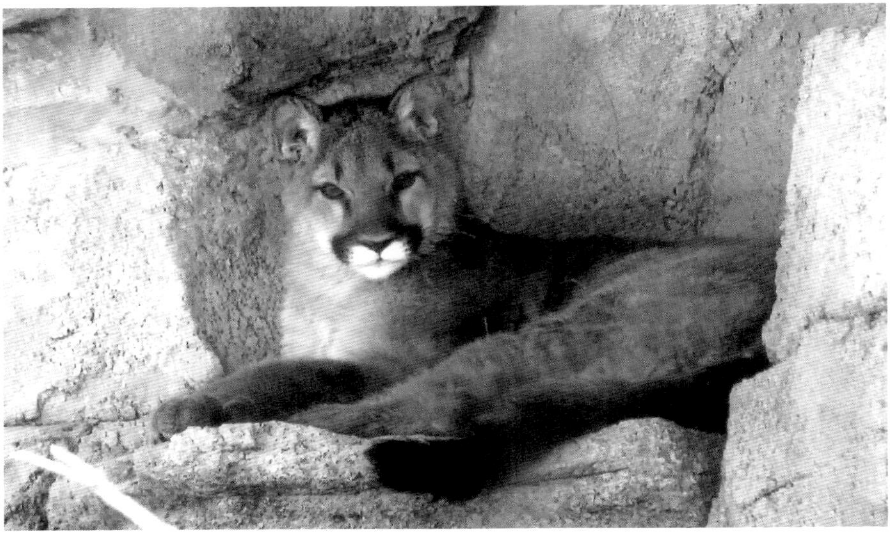

The elusive mountain lion prefers to live in the craggy ledges of the high country in the Guadalupe Mountains. The beautiful cat, known by many names, including cougar, puma, painter, catamount and panther, is the second-heaviest cat in the New World, with the jaguar being the first. *Author's collection.*

The turkey was the only bird the Ndé found significant enough to eat, but there is evidence that dove, quail and pigeons were also eaten and the feathers used for arrows.

The Guadalupe Mountains were home to two great Apache leaders: Victorio, whose native name is Bidu-ya, which means "He Who Checks His Horse," and Geronimo, who was born in June 1829 and whose native name, Goyaalé (or Gokliya), means "One Who Yawns." These two men would prove to be massive thorns in the side of the United States military, leading the troops on many long chases through and around their home territory. The Mexican government would fall victim to their tactics as well.

In 1880, the U.S. Cavalry chased Chief Victorio into the Guadalupe Mountains, where he led them on a long, arduous trek through the treacherous territory. Later that year, in October, Victorio would lose his life in the Tres Castillos Mountains in Chihuahua, Mexico.

McKittrick Canyon was a perfect isolated canyon for the tribes to feel protected against the opposing forces, and it remained that way until the U.S. Army ventured there.

The Mexican government, in an attempt to discourage the Apache from conducting raids in Mexico and to prevent the tribes from settling in the

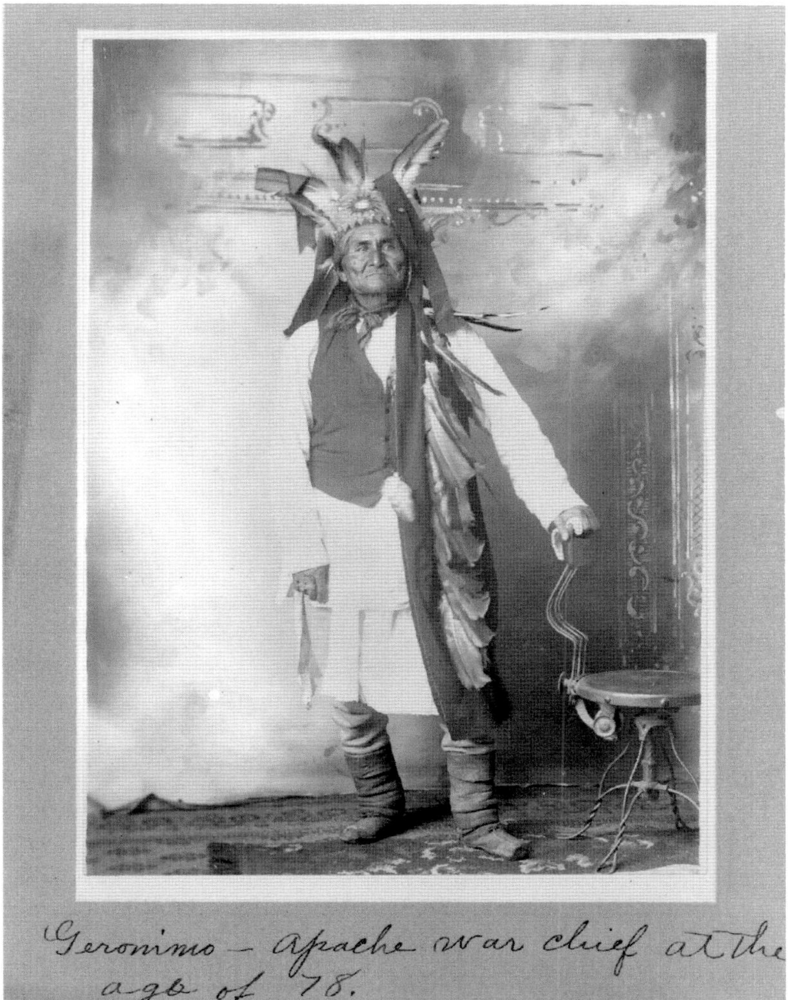

Geronimo, the fierce leader of the Apache, had nine wives in his long life before passing away due to complications from pneumonia brought on by a horse-riding accident one year after this photograph was taken. *Courtesy Library of Congress.*

southern regions, put a $100 bounty on Apache male scalps, a $50 bounty on a woman's scalp and a $25 bounty on a child's. This enraged the natives, who had never scalped their enemy. But afterward, for every Apache scalp taken, the horrible trophy of war was avenged tenfold by the grief-stricken tribe.

Geronimo and his mother, who were living in southwestern New Mexico near present-day Santa Rita, narrowly missed a terrible massacre when a man known as James Johnson, who had befriended the tribe of Mangus Colorado (Red Sleeves), made many promises of great things upon his return from a trip north to Santa Fe but instead brought with him death and destruction in the form of a military cannon, or howitzer, filled with chain, nails and scrap iron. Reportedly, this killed four to five hundred of the young warrior's tribe, mostly women and children. Johnson and his men then scalped the dead and took them to Mexico for their reward.

Hatred for the white people and the Mexicans was cemented with this terrible act of cruelty. This one horrendous tragedy would ultimately cost the American settlers more lives, as Apache hearts were now filled with revenge and rage toward anyone who resembled those who perpetrated or encouraged this crime, innocent or not.

The Apaches were in an unenviable, precarious spot—not only was their homeland slowly being overrun with white settlers, who wanted the natives out, but the Mexicans to the south were paying for their scalps as well. Forced to stay on the move, the tribe developed fierce war skills and fought to the death for their culture.

By 1987, under the direction of Texas Tech anthropologists Paul and Susana Katz, who have done phenomenal work in the fields of archaeology and anthropology in the Guadalupe Mountains of both Texas and New Mexico as well as many other regions, the number of recorded archaeological sites had risen to 299, 29 of which met the criteria for entrance into the National Register of Historic Places.

Although the Mescalero Apache tribe is now located mainly in the Sacramento Mountains, influences of their culture are still felt in the Guadalupes. One example is the annual Mescal Roast that occurs every May at the Guadalupe Mountains National Park Visitors' Center. This event celebrates the culture of the Mescalero while educating visitors on their rich traditions. The Living Desert Zoo and Gardens State Park in Carlsbad, New Mexico, had a long-standing tradition of hosting the Mescal Roast but after twenty-six years reluctantly turned over the reins of this special event to the Guadalupe Mountains National Park due to staffing issues. The Living Desert still serves as a venue for Native American vendors to show their handiwork in the visitors' center, as it still holds a valued relationship with the tribes represented during the show.

The Guadalupe Mountains have always been a sacred spot for the Mescalero Apache tribes as the birthplace of their culture, and this is a tradition the current caretaker of the mountains, the National Park Service, values and respects.

CHAPTER 3

MILITARY PRESENCE

As white settlers began to push west, native people pushed back. The U.S. government was not tolerant of or patient with the native populations and began to force them off the land that they and their families had considered theirs for thousands of years.

Atrocities occurred on both sides, and many American military campaigns were sent to the region with one main mission: eliminate the Apache tribe from the Guadalupes. The Ninth and Tenth Cavalry, commonly known as the Buffalo Soldiers, were sent to Pine Springs, Texas, where the stage station for the Butterfield Stage Line was located. These soldiers fought bravely against the native tribes, who gave these black soldiers their name. The buffalo, or bison, which once appeared in "swarms" its numbers were so large, was an important animal for the tribes, who viewed it as not only a provider for nearly every aspect of their lives but also as a symbol of strength and stamina. When the natives saw the way the black soldiers fought, they were impressed and gave them the moniker.

The Buffalo Soldiers were sent to eradicate the native population and secure the region by rounding up the citizens to be placed in reservations. Many bloody battles occurred between the U.S. Army and the Mescalero Apache tribes in or near McKittrick Canyon. It has long been commented how ironic it is that some of the very people who had just earned their freedom from slavery were commissioned to force another race into that same fate.

Armed conflict over land held by the native tribes became commonplace. At first, the U.S. Army had imagined the western expansion as an easy task, meeting with little resistance, but this was not the case once the mission began. The new recruits were to come up against a new type of warrior—one with excellent guerrilla tactics and one who knew how to attack fast and depart before his prey realized what had happened.

Victorio, an Apache leader, was causing trouble for the western settlers and United States government in 1867, so the military sent in the Tenth Cavalry Buffalo Soldiers to remove him from the area by whatever means necessary. Another chief, known as Cadete, Volunteer or, in his native tongue, Gian-na-tah, which means "always ready," played an important role in trying to unite the Apache with the Comanche while conducting negotiations with the Anglos.

According to a plaque at the Manzanita Springs massacre site, First Lieutenant Howard Bass Cushing, a young officer with the U.S. Army, was a "most daring, gallant and reckless Indian fighter" in his approach to rid the Guadalupe Mountains of the Mescalero Apache. The Mescalero might disagree with the "gallant" part of Cushing's description, however, based on the following passage from the plaque (quotes are attributed to Cushing):

> *This refuge was invaded when, from behind the boulders on the lower slopes before you, a fire of rifle shot signaled the start of Cushing's raid. "Abandoning everything but their ponies, they* [the Mescalero] *rapidly scaled the steep slopes in scattered parties, driving their stock ahead of them." Dead horses and mules rolled down the mountainside. "Keeping some of my men after the Indians, I put others to work to destroy the rancheria." They* [Cushing's men] *burned immense numbers of buffalo robes, tanned beef, deer and antelope skins, 20,000 pounds of prepared mescal, and 15,000 pounds of jerked beef. Indian saddles were added to the flames in such large numbers they were not even counted. Twenty-five "wigwams," clothing, bows and arrows, cooking utensils, and liquor were either burned or carried off. "By hard labor, a little after dark, the destruction was complete," especially for the Apache people depending on this winter cache.*

A "thin plume of smoke" had alerted Cushing and his men to the existence of Cadete's Apache camp in McKittrick Canyon in December 1869. This discovery would lead to the death and wounding of over fifty Apache and the destruction of the winter supplies for the surviving few. This branch of the canyon was called Sanguinara by Cushing.

Cadete survived this attack but was convinced to surrender his tribe to Colonel Christopher "Kit" Carson and the U.S. government in the

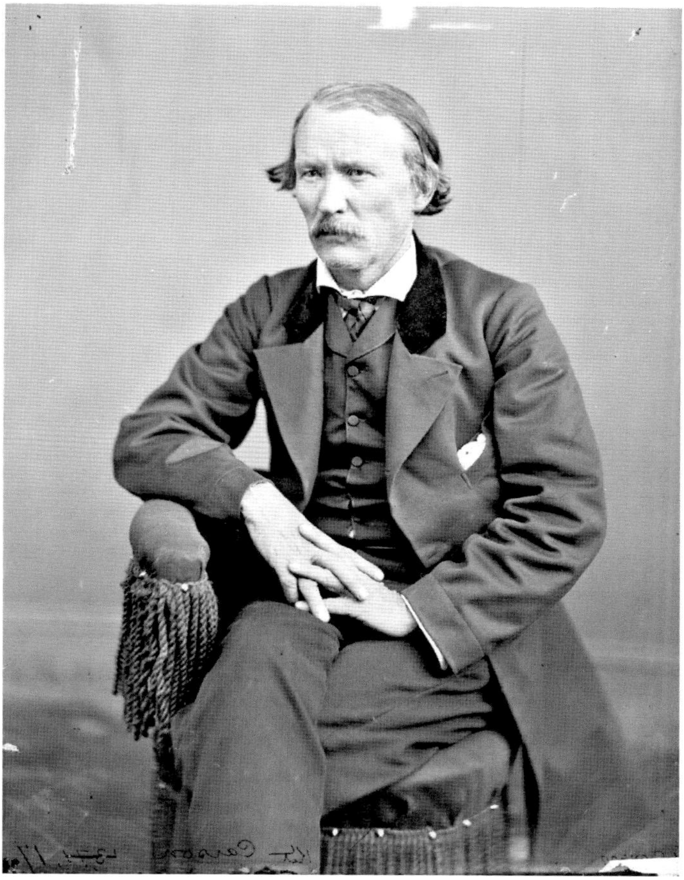

Christopher "Kit" Carson served as a courier and scout during the Mexican-American War and participated in the pursuit of the Navajo, Mescalero Apache, Kiowa and Comanche tribes. He became a controversial character after his participation in forcing the Navajo tribe to relocate to the Bosque Redondo in Fort Sumner, New Mexico, more readily known as the Long Walk since it was over three hundred miles from their native home in northern New Mexico and Arizona. *Courtesy Library of Congress.*

summer of 1871 at the Bosque Redondo in Fort Sumner, New Mexico. His was the first tribe to be incarcerated. An eloquent speaker, Cadete shared his views as a broken warrior during this surrender:

> *You* [the Anglos] *are stronger than we. We have fought you so long as we had rifles and powder; but your weapons are better than ours. Give us our*

> *weapons and turn us loose, and we will fight you again. But we are worn out; we have no more heart; we have no provisions, no means to live; your troops are everywhere; our springs and water holes are occupied by your young men. You have driven us from our last and best stronghold, and we have no more heart. Do with us as may seem good to you, but do not forget that we are men.*

Cadete was not happy to have his people surrender, as he did not believe the white ways were the best for his people. His point was illustrated perfectly when the U.S. government began to "modernize" the tribe by means of haircuts, new clothes and an abolishment of their native language. Cadete and his tribe fought back with actions and words. In the following passage, he relays his thoughts to Captain John C. Cremony, a journalist fluent in the Apache dialect:

> *You desire our children to learn from books, and say, that because you have done so, you are able to build all those big houses, and sail over the sea, and talk with each other at any distance, and do many wonderful things; now, let me tell you what we think. You begin when you are little to work hard, and work until you are men in order to begin fresh work. You say that you work in order to learn how to work well. After you get to be men, then you say, the labor of life commences; then too, you build big houses, big ships, big towns, and everything else in proportion. Then, after you got them all, you die and leave them all behind. Now, we call that slavery. You are slaves from the time you begin to talk until you die; but we are as free as air. We never work, but the Mexicans and others work for us. Our wants are few and easily supplied. The river, the wood and plain yield all that we require, and we will not be slaves; nor will we send our children to your schools, where they only learn to become like yourselves.*

Cadete would unfortunately suffer a mortal wound in an ambush during a peace mission in 1872.

In 1870, a group of soldiers from Fort Quitman, under the command of Major Albert Morrow, joined several other regiments from Forts Davis and Stockton to scour the Guadalupe Mountains for renegade members of the Mescalero Apache tribe. During this mission, the troops entered McKittrick Canyon and quickly became lost. In his journal, Morrow wrote the following about the incident:

> *The guides knew nothing of the country we were now in, but* [I] *again took up the trail and after marching four or five hours found myself back in the camp of the night before. In this march, we passed about two hundred recently occupied lodges...Our guides, although the best in the country, were completely baffled by the multiplicity of trails running in every direction, crossing and retracing. They finally succeeded in finding a trail leading down what appeared to be an impassable ravine; the horses and pack mules had to be lifted over the rocks. One or two fell into crevices and could not be extricated. Toward evening we came across a rancheria of 75 lodges which the Indians abandoned at our approach, leaving a large amount of mezcal* [sic] *bread, about two hundred gallons of an intoxicating beverage brewed from the maguey, and other commissary supplies, and a great number of hides, robes, and all sorts of utensils and furniture pertaining to an Indian village.*

In another incident, the troops came across another large Apache rancheria. Unfortunately for the native tribe, the troops completed the mission they were entrusted with and destroyed the settlement "with great enthusiasm," according to the Texas State Historical Society.

Yet another such story illustrates the callous attitude, or possibly the utter eagerness to complete their assigned duties, of the soldiers of that era. A group of soldiers came upon a large settlement of Apache late one evening in the Guadalupe Mountains but decided to wait until the following morning to act. As the unsuspecting tribe began to wake in the morning and make breakfast, the military group attacked. Every member of the tribe was killed, and to add insult to injury, the military proceeded to eat the food the tribe had started to prepare before the attack.

Of course, the whites weren't the only ones committing such atrocities. Known as a brutal tribe, the Comanche were especially relentless in their pursuit of other tribes and the settlers who were beginning to move into the area in large numbers. These actions led to the formation of the so-called Comanche War Trail, where strongholds such as Fort Davis, Texas, and Fort Stockton, Texas, were built in order to protect the settlers, travelers and mail carriers. Wagons of settlers and soldiers alike were found burned on the very spot where they were attacked. The victims suffered many gruesome wounds, as the Comanche made sure they suffered greatly before the relief of death. You can still find evidence of these attacks in the area today.

The U.S. soldiers were used to waging battles out in the open and on flat ground, but the native tribesmen were experts in finding ways to elude the army by setting up fortresses in the mountains and forcing the troops to follow them there. The Guadalupe Mountains provided a perfect shelter from the invading troops, and the tribes would conduct raids on the surrounding and mostly unsuspecting settlers from a definite vantage point. McKittrick Canyon proved to be one of the most treacherous canyons for the military to navigate, according to its records.

Several spent cartridges from a Spencer rifle have been found near the mouth of McKittrick Canyon, leading researchers to believe that there were several battles between Apaches and U.S. soldiers fought in that location. The Spencer, a seven-shot repeating carbine, was used by both sides of the Civil War, although it was especially popular with the Union cavalry because of its light weight. However, it is believed that the Apache were armed with them as well, since spent cartridges were found mixed in with the artifacts scattered in the early camps. Developed by Christopher Spencer in 1860, the rifle was the turning point of the battles between the two dissimilar cultures.

Once reservations were established and the U.S. government was satisfied that the "Indian problems" were sufficiently under control, military presence in the area was diminished, and troops were used in other skirmishes to follow. The Guadalupe Mountains have not seen an Apache presence living within their protection since.

CHAPTER 4

GOLD TALES

For many years, the romantic notion of great wealth hidden deep within the limestone crevasses of McKittrick Canyon and the Guadalupe Mountains drew prospectors and treasure hunters to the area. One such example is a report of a three-hundred-foot-deep cave, complete with stalagmites and stalactites, in the canyon that is accessible only by a rope. J.C. Hunter Jr. reported that he found the entrance to this mine purely by accident. Hunter marked the entrance and brought his son, Robert, and his foreman's son, Laurie Kincaid, both seventeen at the time, back with some Explorer Scouts from Abilene, Texas, to examine the opening further, but it was empty.

Although gold was the main attraction in the Guadalupe Mountains, copper, calumet and silver were also prevalent and not as elusive as their golden cousin. In McKittrick Canyon, J.C. Hunter Sr. and Matt and Thomas Grisham owned the Grisham-Hunter Prospect, which mined black iron oxides with traces of copper. Several residents of Carlsbad, New Mexico, also staked copper mine claims in the Guadalupes.

No matter which of the following stories you believe, one thing is clear: there is a large cache of extraordinary treasure hidden somewhere in the mystic protection of the Guadalupe Mountains. But beware—this treasure might come with a huge price.

Ben Sublett

One of the best-known gold tales involves Texas prospector William Column "Ben" Sublett, who would emerge from the Guadalupes with a pouch of gold nuggets on his belt on a regular basis. Sublett was described as a whiskey-drinking, tobacco-chewing character who would spend weeks at a time in the Guadalupe Mountains, especially McKittrick Canyon, at what he said was an Apache gold mine.

Sublett, who lived in Odessa, Texas, in the 1880s, a time when it was a mere tent city/railroad construction camp, made a meager living repairing windmills and working as a "witcher" using a divining rod or willow branch to locate water wells along the right of way for the Texas & Pacific Railroad. A frequent patron of Mollie William's Saloon in Odessa, Sublett would sit for hours telling his tall tales of fabulous gold to anyone who would listen. The only problem was that he had a family at home living in squalid conditions. The gold mine consumed Sublett, who was known to go away from home for weeks at a time and leave his young children, two girls and a boy, to their own devices. Concerned citizens helped the children the best they could, but the Subletts were raised not to accept charity. The eldest daughter would bring in money by doing laundry for their neighbors. It was only occasionally that Sublett would bring home a nugget or two to help with the children's basic needs. In today's society, their fate would have been much different.

After many years of this pattern, Sublett rolled his wagon up to the door of Mollie William's Saloon, walked into the bar (with a heavy limp due to an old bullet wound) and loudly announced that he had finally found the gold mine he had been looking for. He added, "I have been poor, but I ain't poor no longer. I can buy out this whole town and still have plenty left. Drink!" The barkeep was skeptical until Sublett produced a small buckskin pouch filled with gold nuggets. These nuggets would supply the entire bar with a fun-filled evening accented with much alcohol. "I have at last found the richest gold mine in the world," said Sublett. "I can build a palace of California marble and buy up the entire state of Texas as a backyard for my children to play in." Although Sublett never built that palace, it is said that he never worked again after his gold discovery. Apparently, Ben enjoyed displaying his treasure more than anything and did not spend it on frivolous items like homes and land.

Many people begged Sublett to show them where the mine was located; Texas cowman George Gray even offered him $10,000 to let him accompany him on a mining trip. Sublett replied, "Why? I could go out and dig that much in less than a week." But Gray was not fully deterred by Sublett's remarks, so he hired a gentleman by the name of Jim Flannigan to follow the old prospector the next time he took off toward his treasure. When the time came a few weeks later, Flannigan followed Sublett's burro-drawn wagon for a total of seventy-five miles before he lost the prospector's trail completely. Sublett had already gone to his destination, acquired his loot and returned while Flannigan was still going in circles in the Guadalupe foothills. Several other people would attempt to follow Sublett, but they, too, failed.

Sublett actually did tell a few people how to find the mine. One of the lucky prospectors, Mike Wilson, was successful enough to find the mine and collect a bag of ore, which he then took back to town to celebrate. After Wilson sobered up and attempted to relocate his treasure-trove, however, he was unable to do so. He would spend the rest of his days living in a hut close to the Guadalupes, searching for his lost gold.

Another incident involved two men from Pecos, Texas, who had begged Sublett to take them to the mine for so long that he finally relented. Along the trail to the Guadalupes, however, the old prospector contracted food poisoning. Taking this as a bad sign, and believing his companions were going to do him in when the gold mine was found, Sublett refused to go any farther.

An old, bark-free alligator juniper tree bore nails, symbols and the initials "WCS"—thought to be carved by William Column Sublett—which many said pointed to the mine's opening along the face of the limestone canyon walls. Three symbols were thought to line up with the three cave openings at the mouth of McKittrick. Over the years, the symbols have been removed, so no one is certain as to their true meaning. And although explored many times, the cave yielded no treasures.

Stories of caves filled with Spanish Conquistador armor and golden stirrups have been widely told over the centuries, with several originating from the McKittrick Canyon region. The small caves that litter the canyon could have been used by the early explorers as shelter or as hiding spots for the victims of roaming tribes.

Texas author J. Frank Dobie illuminates the Sublett story in his book *Coronado's Children*. This one story has probably ignited gold fever for more people than any other—sending many to spend years of their lives searching for the elusive yellow metal hidden so artfully in the bosom of the Guadalupe Mountains.

Later in his life, Sublett took his young son Rolth (sometimes noted as Ross) to the mine location. Since Rolth was between the ages of nine and fifteen, he remembered few details about his trip, which most likely occurred in 1887. Rolth vaguely remembered traveling by wagon for an extended length of time

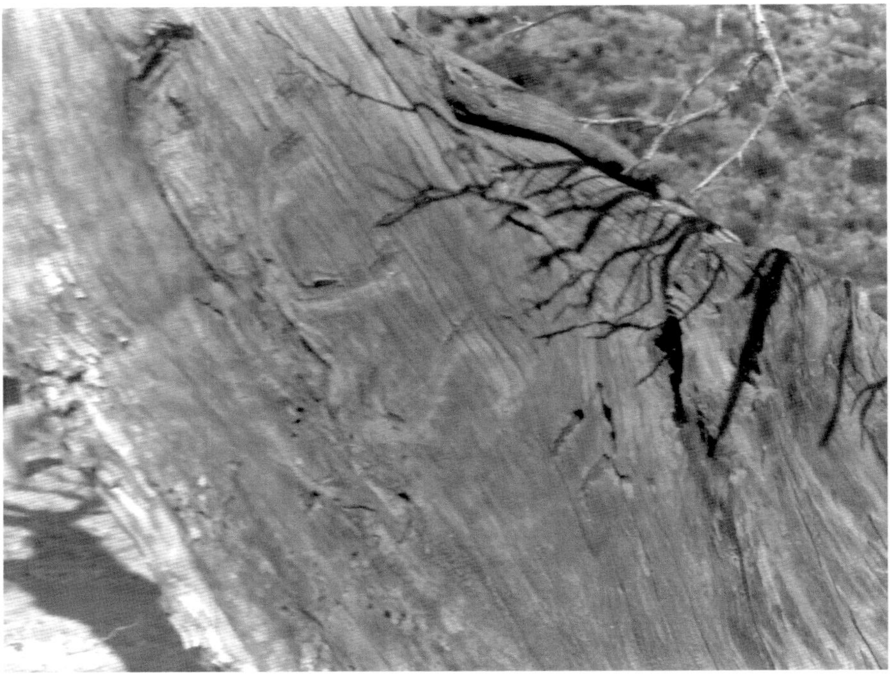

An alligator juniper with the initials "WCS" carved into the bark, widely thought to have been placed there by prospector William Column "Ben" Sublett during one of his many expeditions in the pursuit of gold in the Guadalupe Mountains. This tree was located at the mouth of McKittrick Canyon. *Courtesy of Guadalupe Mountains National Park.*

and that when they finally reached their destination, a nearby pool of water distracted the youth from observing the exact location. His most vivid memory was of his father descending into a crevice or cave by means of a rope ladder, from which he extracted a large quantity of gold nuggets. As a child, this did not mean too much to Rolth, but as he grew, he realized the value of the knowledge. The elder Sublett was not so accommodating to his son's newfound interest in the mine: "If you want to know, you have to look for it like I did."

The exact location of this vast treasure was lost in 1892 with the death of Ben Sublett, who was apparently "taking it with him." Those who tried to follow in Sublett's footsteps would systematically say they found the treasure, enter into giddy euphoria and then meet a tragic death before being able to share their good fortune or the exact location of the gold. Some say the "Curse of the Guadalupes" is responsible.

Shortly after Sublett's death, a Carlsbad sheriff, Cicero Stewart, went looking for the gold mine and came upon a cowboy named Grizzly Bill,

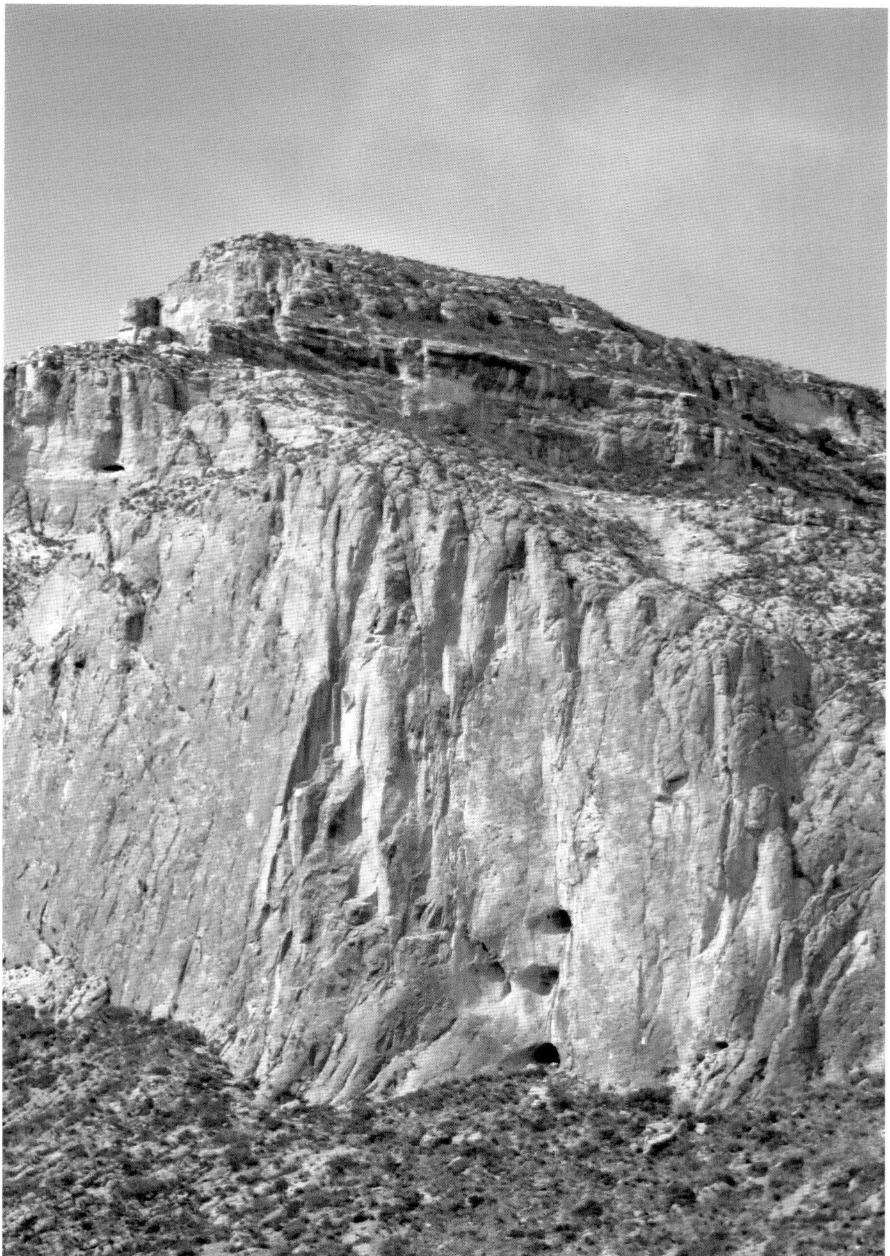

Depressions in the stone face of the north wall of McKittrick Canyon are said to have been a landmark used by prospector Sublett to locate his fabled gold mine. *Author's collection.*

who bragged that he had just found the treasure and was going to his Pecos, Texas home to show it off. After creating quite a scene in a local saloon by shooting his six-shooter and yelling at the top of his lungs, Grizzly Bill began drinking heavily, spending his nuggets and acting extremely foolish. His last act was to attempt to ride a wild horse while drunk. This resulted in a broken neck and death for Grizzly Bill, and the world was no closer to having knowledge of the gold mine.

On his deathbed, Rolth Sublett gave a note to a friend indicating the location of the lost gold mine. Legend states that the friend never used the knowledge and took the secret to the grave.

Many authors have speculated that this fabulous treasure was possibly the booty from a stage heist, but others believe that it was a true gold mine, given the fact that ropes were necessary in the apprehension of the gold. It is a true mystery in an equally mysterious place that might never be solved.

Lucius Arthur

Lucius Arthur's story began as he overheard a conversation between two Mexican men in an Ysleta, Texas tavern about a magnificent gold mine in the Guadalupe Mountains. One of the men was known to have come into some riches and was living very well, especially when compared to his sheepherder beginnings. The men made reference to a hole in a mountain with more gold than they could ever spend, and it was then that Arthur decided to follow them on their next journey.

The men eventually left on horses and were leading burros with supplies. Unprepared and unsure of the distance he would have to travel, Arthur reluctantly turned back. Several months later, the men made another trek into the Guadalupes with Arthur—this time fully prepared—close behind. From a safe distance, an amazed Arthur observed the men as they descended into a crevice and produced several bags of not only ore but also water for their livestock and themselves. The men took their fill of ore and water and returned to Ysleta, leaving Arthur the possibility to explore the site further.

The mine was a deep cavern in a canyon that, by his estimate, dropped about three hundred feet. Although he was prepared with foodstuffs and other traveling necessities, he had not brought a long enough rope to allow him to explore the mine more fully. A ledge of pure silver rimmed the walls of a deep chasm. From this ledge, Arthur was able to pull several large specimens of the precious metal before returning to town. Once in town, he secured a length of rope he thought would be sufficient to transport him down into the cave.

With his supplies in hand, Arthur traveled back to the spot where he thought the treasure-trove was located; however, it was said that he was unable to find his life-changing metal once he returned, and he would never be seen again.

Was it the Curse of the Guadalupes taking another victim, or did Arthur find enough gold to never have to return to Ysleta, Texas, again? We will probably never know.

BEN WATSON

Here is where it gets confusing. In his March 9, 1967 "Tolbert's Texas" article in the *Dallas Morning News*, Frank Tolbert wrote about an odd gold story concerning another old prospector known as "Uncle Ben" Watson. Two Bens with treasure tales in the same mountains certainly keeps researchers on their toes. According to Tolbert, Ben Watson had reportedly found the lost Ben Sublett mine and was, like his predecessor, keeping the location to himself.

Watson, who called himself "a crazy old prospector," was also a part of a more elaborate tale involving an old quart milk bottle that was found north of Fabens, Texas, at the location of a former stage stop. The bottle contained a piece of chamois cloth on which was drawn a map, was sealed with a cork made from a mesquite branch and was wrapped with a strip of lechuguilla string. An image of El Capitan was hand-inked onto the cloth, surrounded by arrows and the word "gold." Dated May 11, 1901, the map was signed by Ben Watson and instructed the lucky finder to give it to the State of Texas with a promise that the state would reward the finder greatly.

Found next to the bottle was a three-sided rock with crude symbols carved onto its surface, including an image of El Capitan and the words "silver mine," "guns," "dead Indians" and "camp" highlighted by arrows indicating the approximate location for each label.

It was widely rumored—mostly due to Watson's own boasting—that the prospector had bored tunnels through the base of El Capitan. This would be a monumental task, to say the least—especially since the mountain is solid limestone. No evidence has been found of his reported efforts, but it would have been possible for him to create a mine of some distance.

The fact that the Guadalupe Mountains are composed almost solely of limestone causes most to believe that gold would not be found as a vein to be mined (although silver and copper can be mined from the mountains). Thus, treasure hunters tend to think that the gold found by Watson and others was actually outlaw caches that had been spirited away by the Apache. Except for the purposes of trade, the native tribes placed no real value on gold, though they learned quickly to use it to their advantage by exchanging a small amount of gold stone to supply themselves with rifles and ammunition.

Ben Watson was a flamboyant character who haunted the Guadalupe Mountains in life and is rumored to still be there in death. He normally wore white-striped bib overalls and would keep his brilliantly white hair shoulder length, as he had sworn off barbers many years earlier. Known for his metal

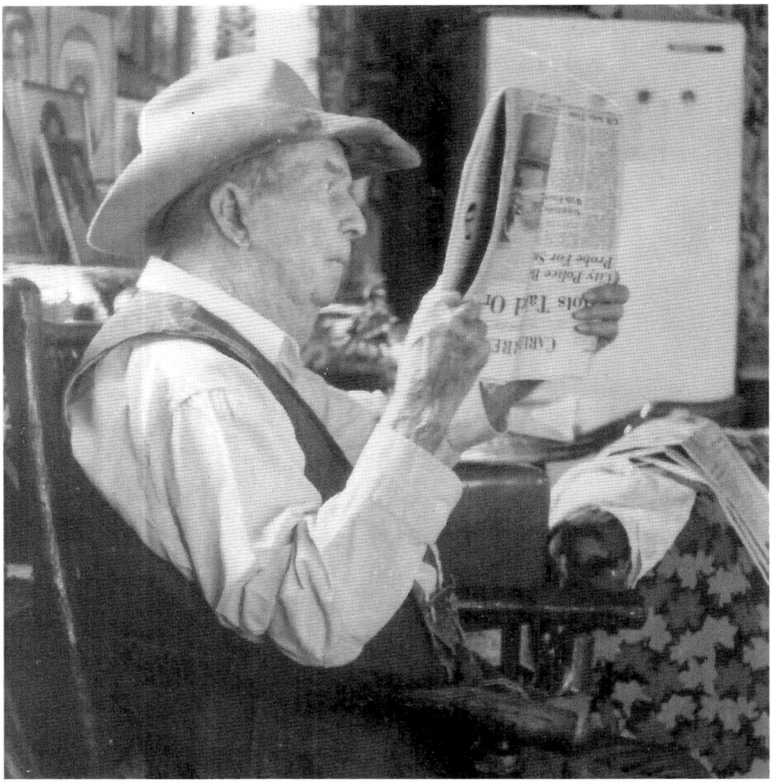

While ranching in the area, Walter Glover became privy to many gold tales that involved the Guadalupe Mountains. Many people would gather at Glover's store to drink coffee and hear the latest gossip. *Courtesy Guadalupe Mountains National Park.*

hook hand, Watson never let a disability hold him back from prospecting in his beloved Guadalupe Mountains. Although he claimed to be over one hundred years old, he trounced around in the Guadalupe Mountains like he was in his thirties.

Walter Glover, owner of the Pine Springs Store, would delight visitors and locals alike with his tales of great riches hidden in the Guadalupe Mountains. Glover also knew Watson and his wife, who were residents of Pine Springs, Texas, as well. Glover told fanciful tales of outlaws who would hurriedly stash their ill-gotten bounty in the many caves dotted in the Guadalupe Mountains in order to avoid the treasure being confiscated. These stories tantalized all who heard them, no doubt causing some to catch gold fever.

Because the Butterfield Stage Line traversed the Guadalupe Mountains, its stagecoaches were prime targets for desperados, locals and native tribes and would come through highly armed. Army payroll chests were the most coveted of the shipments wanted by highwaymen. For this reason, the Butterfield Line chose not to carry any large amounts of money, including payroll chests. The only possessions allowed on the stages were those of the passengers, which would sometimes fall victim to the ruffians in a holdup situation.

Toward the end of his life, Watson told Hunter Ranch foreman Noel Kincaid, "I know where the entrances to the tunnels in the mine are, and the tunnel is big enough for a man and a jackass to walk through. Only I'm not telling. The world's not ready for that gold mine."

Sadly, Watson took the location of the fabulous gold mine to his grave.

Abijha (or Elijah) Long

After the Butterfield Stage Line discontinued business, Wells Fargo took up the line, and it, too, experienced holdups by waiting outlaws and ruffians looking for an easy mark. One of the company's strongboxes was reported to be found in the early 1920s by local guano miner Abijha (or Elijah) "Ed" Long, who also claimed to have explored what would become the Carlsbad Caverns before Jim White. This is a debate that still rages on in Carlsbad, New Mexico.

Accounts tell of how Long discovered a Wells Fargo strongbox containing an estimated $30,000 in gold bullion near Pine Springs Canyon while working for the Walter Glover Ranch, several canyons away from

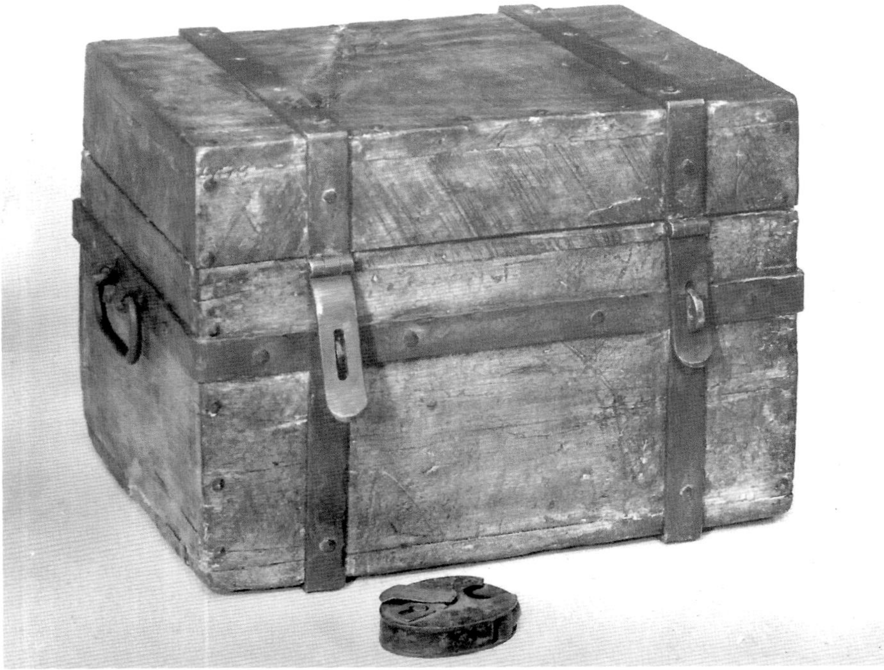

This strongbox, which was found in the Pine Springs, Texas area, was said to have contained $30,000 in gold coins. The box is now housed in the Smithsonian Museum. *Author's collection.*

McKittrick. Long consigned the fortune to himself in California and promptly vanished.

Since the money and strongbox had originally belonged to Wells Fargo, the company conducted an investigation into the circumstances behind the find. After an exhaustive analysis of the facts, Wells Fargo concluded that there had been no wrongdoing and dropped the case.

Long was later found living on his cattle ranch in Oregon, which he purchased with the proceeds from the sale of the $30,000 in gold for a whopping $90,000. After Mr. Long relinquished the strongbox to Wells Fargo, it was placed in the Smithsonian, where it remains today.

Goat Herder's Tale

Another story of great wealth was told by a goat herder named Jesse Duran, who was employed by J.C. Hunter Sr. In the spring of 1930, while looking for one of his lost charges within the farthest eastern limits of the Hunter Ranch, Duran stumbled upon a small cave. Three skeletal, partially clothed soldiers peered back at him as he investigated the opening. Unsettled by his discovery, Duran did not enter the cave but instead took a visual inventory of what the soldiers were guarding: a cache of rifles, gold coins, silver bars and three strongboxes that appeared to be like the ones used by Wells Fargo—all of which he could have used to make a better life for him and his family, who had just recently migrated from Mexico. However, being taught as a child to never disturb the dead, Duran was afraid that if he were to remove any of the treasures, he would bring the wrath of the three soldiers down on him and his family. Shaken, he relayed the incredible find to Frank Stogden and a couple other ranchers, including Hunter Ranch foreman Noel Kincaid, who were playing cards at Stogden's home. The ranchers insisted that Duran show them exactly where the opening was immediately, but Jesse refused to do so.

Stogden allowed Duran to rest in his barn until the next day, hoping that the young man would agree to help them in their pursuit. When they checked on him that morning, however, he had vanished, and he was never seen in the Guadalupe Mountains again. (Duran later showed up in California, where he worked until his death in the 1970s.) Not to be dissuaded by the goat herder's absence, the ranchers went to the area that Duran had described the night before, but even with extensive searches, they were unable to find the magnificent treasure he had described.

Word of Duran's discovery spread quickly throughout the region, and before long, Rader Ridge had become a hotbed of treasure-hunting activity. Local Dog Canyon rancher Sam Hughes, who had never heard Duran's story, might have also happened upon the cave opening while deer hunting. Hughes related his discovery to Noel Kincaid, who told him it sounded much like the cave that Jesse Duran had described earlier. In true fashion, when the pair attempted to locate the opening again, they were unsuccessful.

This cave appears to be the same one described in a 1924 *Frontier Times* magazine article that details a very similar opening and gold tale told by a cowboy and the daughter of a Mescalero Apache chief. Said to contain some of the finest gold known in the 1870s, the young woman also described it as haunted "with evil spirits of some old race of Indians who lived there years ago and my people are afraid to enter it." The native tribes would not enter the area, but some speculate that this is the same mine that Ben Sublett and Ben Watson stumbled upon later.

Possibly, one day, when the shadows and conditions are correctly aligned, this treasure will reveal itself once again to an unsuspecting individual. But until then, it still belongs to the Guadalupe Mountains.

Geronimo's Gold

In order to allow further progression by the white settlers into the West, the United States government decided that the Apache, Comanche and Navajo tribes had to be controlled. This attitude did not sit well with the tribes and their leaders, causing some of them to revolt. One such revolutionary was Mescalero Apache chief Geronimo.

After his eventual capture, Geronimo was said to have whispered a tale of great riches to some of the soldiers, indicating that he had knowledge of the "richest gold mine in the western world," located in the Guadalupe Mountains. In exchange for the freedom of his people, Geronimo stated that he was willing to divulge the mine's location to the U.S. Army.

Apache tribes were occasionally observed by both settlers and the military to wear silver jewelry sometimes adorned with gold—this gold was rumored to have come from the lost gold mine in McKittrick Canyon.

Once again, the curse took hold, and Geronimo was to die without the treasure revealing itself to the world.

A New Mexico Governor's Tale

The Guadalupe Mountains also garnered interest from Civil War general and appointed governor of New Mexico Lew Wallace. The author of *Ben-Hur* and pen pal of outlaw Billy the Kid, Wallace was also credited with igniting interest in the lost Guadalupe Mountains gold mine when he reported finding an old piece of yellowed paper on the floor in the basement of the Governor's Palace in Santa Fe, New Mexico, while it was being remodeled.

Legend has it that the ancient Spanish document revealed how, during one of the many Spanish entradas, a rich gold mine was located in the

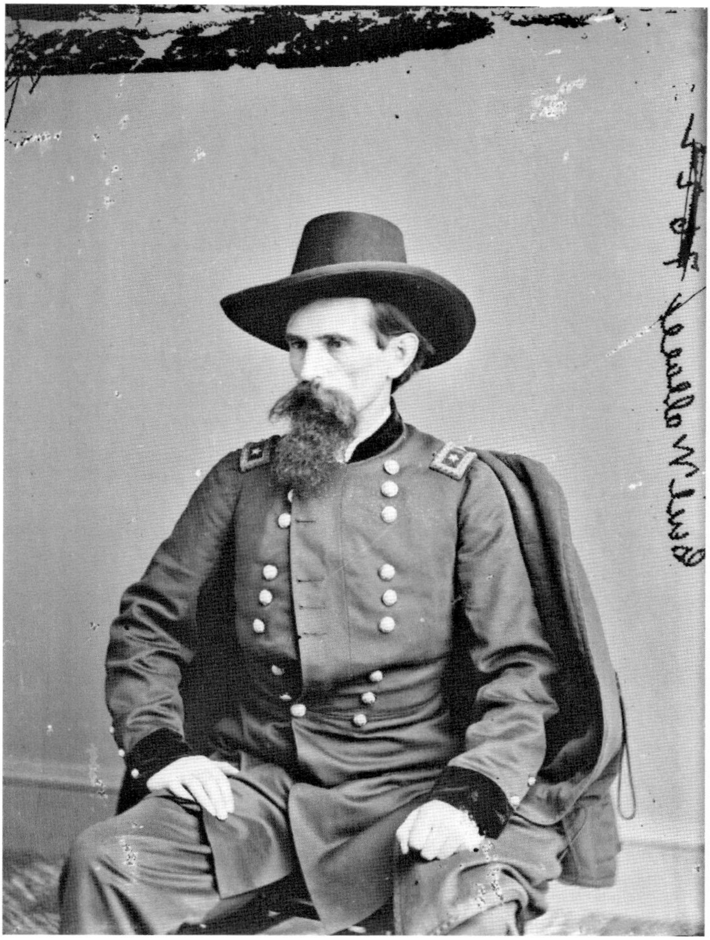

Governor Lew Wallace of New Mexico, author of *Ben-Hur*, created a stir with his claims of finding proof of a gold mine in the Guadalupe Mountains. *Courtesy Library of Congress.*

Sierra de Cenizas (Ashes Mountains) or, as they are known today, the Guadalupe Mountains. The document stated that a converted native from the village of Tabira had acted as a guide for Spaniard Captain de Gavilan and several others who ventured into the Guadalupe Mountains in the early 1600s to look for the legendary gold mine. Apparently, a great treasure was found and celebrated, but this would not last long, as the Pueblo Revolt of 1680 all but eliminated the Spanish population from the territory of New Mexico. Lost along with the lives of the Spaniards was also the knowledge they had about the vast riches. The Pueblo people destroyed everything the Spanish had brought to the New World, including churches, books and personal items; they wanted no reminders of their oppressors.

Curse of the Guadalupes

The Curse of the Guadalupes, whether truth or superstition, has taken its toll on those few foolish, gold-drunk individuals who squandered their fortunes, all the while quietly rewarding those who were less greedy. It is said the native tribes put a death curse on any white man foolish enough to try his luck in locating a life-changing cache of gold. When asked about the gold tales in his backyard, Noel Kincaid was quoted as saying, "I've lived here [the Guadalupe Mountains] all my life, and I've never found any gold mine. But I've sure found some things to be treasured."

CHAPTER 5
INSTRUMENTAL PLAYERS

Many people worked on the plans for McKittrick Canyon, but six men were by far the most influential of the masses. Without men like Felix McKittrick, Wallace E. Pratt, Noel Kincaid, J.C. Hunter Sr., J.C. Hunter Jr. and Glenn Biggs, the world would probably never have been introduced to the treasures the canyon holds in its current pristine condition.

FELIX MCKITTRICK

According to National Park Service records, rancher Felix McKittrick, namesake of the canyon (a fact that was highly debated for years), bought land at the mouth of the canyon in 1869 and was one of the first Anglo settlers in the Guadalupes. Some of the first records of his existence in the canyon were reported by famed geologist Ralph Silas Tarr, state geologist of Texas and Harvard graduate, during a Guadalupe Mountains symposium in the mid-1890s.

McKittrick was a foreman on the famous Jingle-Bob Ranch of cattleman John Simpson Chisum in Texas and also near Roswell, New Mexico, where he was a well-respected cowboy, sheriff and Civil War veteran. A member of the Twenty-first Brigade of the Texas State Troops in 1861, McKittrick went on to command the Eighteenth Texas Cavalry (Darnell's Regiment), Cleburne's Division, Hardee's Corps, Army of Tennessee, in 1862. He

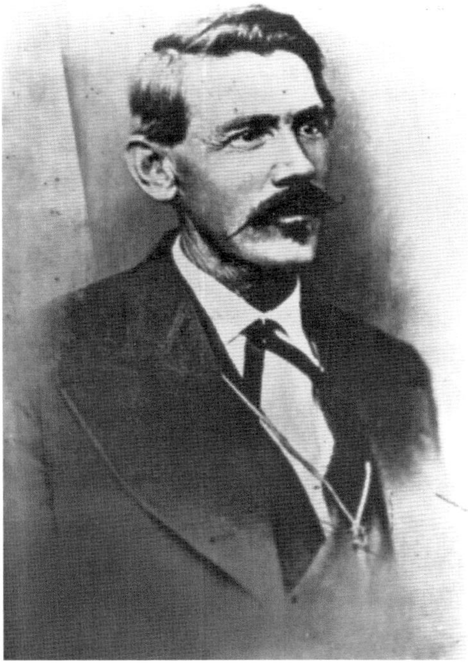

Felix McKittrick worked as a ranch hand for cattle baron John Simpson Chisum in the Roswell, New Mexico region. *Courtesy Southeastern New Mexico Historical Society.*

resigned his rank of captain due to health reasons on November 8, 1862, stating that he was on sick leave more than active duty.

Called "Old Mack" by his employer, John Chisum, McKittrick was one of the first cowboys Chisum hired for his cattle operation and would be a participant on the first cattle drive up the Pecos River in 1867, riding with the likes of a young William H. Bonney (aka Billy the Kid), who was also under Chisum's employ. Chisum would often remark that McKittrick was so much a part of the outfit that he would have to be marked and branded. Chisum's brother, Pitser, was quoted as saying, "Mack would drive a herd of cattle to Egypt if the Comanches would leave him alone."

Prior to the Civil War, McKittrick had served with Captain Mark R. Hardin in Company I, Fourth Regiment of the Kentucky Volunteers, from October 1847 to July 1848 in the Mexican War. The residents of Denton County, Texas, knew McKittrick as their sheriff for a short time before he resigned in 1854. He also worked as a blacksmith early in his life.

Born to Robert "Captain Jack" McKittrick on November 26, 1828, in Washington County, Kentucky, Felix and his elder brother, Fielding, were raised by his aunt China Mitchell after the death of their parents. It was through the sale of his inherited eighty-six acres that Felix was able to move to Texas. Fielding would join a traveling show and never be heard from again. The brothers were the only children of their parents to live past infancy.

Sadly, death would find Felix McKittrick again in 1860 when his wife, Almira Peters, passed away after the birth of their child less than one year after their marriage. Neither mother nor child would survive, and McKittrick would never remarry.

The Civil War would distract McKittrick from his woes for the next few years, as he was involved in some of the largest battles as Texas seceded from the Union and joined the Confederacy in 1861. But once he tendered his resignation, McKittrick traveled west, where he became a cowboy of great fame as he rode for the likes of John Chisum, John Beckwith and Pat Goghlan.

John Tunstall, an English gentleman rancher and friend of Billy the Kid, whose murder would spark the Lincoln County War, loaned Felix money against his crops and also paid the taxes on the McKittrick farm. After participating in the Lincoln County War, McKittrick moved to the Guadalupe Mountains in Texas, where, in 1869, he would acquire the beautiful land that bears his name.

Despite all the tragedy he had endured in his life, McKittrick was known as a prankster with a great sense of humor. Everyone who knew him could count on great stories—most of them true—of Billy the Kid, John Chisum and his life in the wilds of Texas and the New Mexico Territory.

McKittrick, who had had experience growing buckwheat, rye and wheat, supervised the farming on South Spring Ranch and also ran the ranch's commissary. In addition, he conducted farming experiments on his own land, which adjoined Chisum's. Being educated, McKittrick also served as a tutor for the children of Robert Casey, a rancher in the Hondo Valley of New Mexico, as well as performing bookkeeping duties for Casey.

Each rancher had a specific brand or mark that he used to distinguish his livestock from that of his neighbors. The McKittrick cattle had distinctive marks that were hard to ignore. Hornless and earless, each steer was branded with a "6" on its shoulder, side and hip.

While looking for water in the Guadalupe Mountains for the Chisums in 1870, McKittrick recalled a stream in a beautiful canyon he had explored early in his military career, as he had been charged with ridding the Guadalupe Mountains of the Mescalero Apache. McKittrick revisited the canyon, which was to become forever known as McKittrick Canyon in his honor. John Chisum was heard to say on many occasions that the Guadalupes, Sacramentos and El Capitan were a constant inspiration to him because of their strength and beauty.

McKittrick would not live in his canyon for long, however, deciding to move with his business partner, Charley Thomas, to Clifton, Arizona, where he was to have another canyon named after him. Charley Thomas was also a friend of Billy the Kid and rode with him on many occasions. After the death of John S. Chisum and Billy the Kid, McKittrick decided it was time to move on.

McKittrick had suffered at the hands of the native tribes, having had horses stolen from him on a regular basis, and he filed a claim against the United States government to recover his lost monies. The claim for $3,500 was filed for the years 1860, 1870, 1871 and 1877; he would receive a settlement of only $1,680.

While in Clifton, McKittrick and Thomas, who was sometimes known as Charley Thorne, ran a flourishing cattle business and were known to be quite sociable in the community. McKittrick also liked to drink heavily, a habit that would unfortunately lead to his untimely death. During these bouts with the bottle, McKittrick loved to tell stories to the good people of Clifton—whether factual or fantasy—about his days as a cowboy on the Jingle-Bob Ranch, his exploits with outlaw Billy the Kid and his days as a fierce Indian fighter. He is said to have been quite a storyteller, becoming more enthusiastic with every drink he finished.

One story he liked to tell involved Billy the Kid, a friend of both McKittrick and Chisum. Feelings changed, however, when Chisum reneged on a promise to pay Billy $500 to keep rustlers away from the Chisum cattle. This story showed the extent of these hard feelings. According to McKittrick, four Jingle-Bob cowboys had settled in for the night during a roundup when they were surprised by Billy, who proceeded to kill three of the four and was said to have relayed this chilling message to the survivor: "Tell him [Chisum] I am living now to get even with my enemies. I shall kill his men whenever I find them and credit him with $5 for each man I kill. Whenever I see him [Chisum], I intend to kill him, and then I will call the account square."

Many thought that Chisum himself had started this tale of retaliation to evoke fear of Billy and get rid of him for good. Billy's good friend Patrick F. Garrett was either "elected" or hired by Chisum, depending on who you talk to, to rid New Mexico of the outlaw—a task he completed on July 14, 1881, in Fort Sumner, New Mexico. Tensions were high at the ranch until news of Billy's death was delivered.

Felix McKittrick, himself, would suffer a tragic end to an equally tragic life. His death notice in the March 8, 1901 *Arizona Bulletin* explained the circumstances of the much-loved pioneer's passing:

> *An Old Western Pioneer Meets a Sudden Death—Drowned in Blue River Near His Home—22nd Day of February.*

> *How long he had been dead when found is a matter of conjecture, but as* [r]*igor mortis had set in his death must have occurred sometime before his body was found by a passerby. McKittrick is described as a man of fine intelligence and good education who volunteered as a soldier in the Mexican War and was discharged from the army with a fine record. Fought for the South in Civil War and believed in "democracy as taught and promulgated by the founders of our Republic." McKittrick moved to Arizona to conduct business with cattle. Never closed his door to a stranger or traveler, he was very hospitable—no one ever left his cabin hungry.*

Another article written by Tom Pickett of Clifton, Arizona, stated:

> *McKittrick moved on to Clifton and settled on the Blue River. He would drink a lot and tell stories of Billy the Kid, Chisum, etc. and brought Charley Thomas/Thorne with him to Arizona. One night after drinking heavily at a neighbor's house, McKittrick took his two-mule buckboard home—crossed the Blue River where the bank was steep. The front wheel of the rig hit a rock—pitched him forward over the top of the buckboard. His legs or clothes got caught on something and his head hung down into the water—he was found drowned in this position. The mules had not moved.*

According to burial records, McKittrick's grave is the oldest in the cemetery. There is a marker on the bank of the Blue River at the spot where McKittrick lost his life. James McKittrick, a relative, would write to the *Carlsbad Current-Argus* about the character of Felix McKittrick in 1965 and whether the canyon was actually named for Felix. "Surely this man must have had some strong attribute which caused his name to be stamped on so many places where he must have ridden," he wrote.

J.C. Hunter Sr.

Jesse Coleman Hunter, known to his friends as J.C., moved to the region in 1911 to become the school superintendent for Van Horn, Texas, which is about eighty miles away from the Guadalupe Mountains. As an oilman of considerable wealth and avid sportsman, Hunter became aware of the opportunity in the Guadalupe Mountains and worked toward buying land there. By 1925, Hunter owned forty-three thousand acres in the Guadalupe

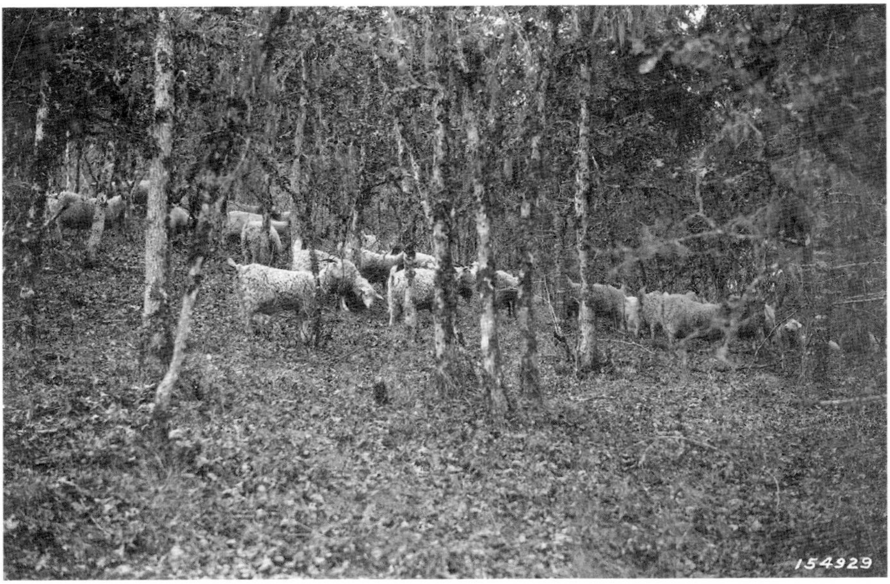

J.C. Hunter Sr., who ran Angora goats in McKittrick Canyon as a cash producer, lost many of his herd to the black bears that roamed the canyon. *Courtesy Wikimedia.*

Mountains, including McKittrick Canyon, where he ran four thousand Angora goats.

A field trip to the newly promoted Carlsbad Caverns and McKittrick Canyon in 1925 was attended by one hundred dignitaries, including Texas governor Pat Neff, highway commissioners from both Texas and New Mexico and members of the Texas State Parks Board. J.C. Hunter was proud to show off his land and the potential it held, thus planting the seed of future development of the area.

In 1928, Hunter hosted a twenty-four-hour picnic at his line shack in McKittrick Canyon and played host to over five hundred dignitaries. This ignited interest in turning both McKittrick Canyon and the Guadalupe Mountains into the "recreation center of Texas." The proposed recreational park was not to materialize in McKittrick Canyon, but the highway from Carlsbad, New Mexico, to El Paso, Texas, did result from this meeting.

Ever the consummate oilman, Hunter acquired 43,200 acres between the New Mexico and Texas borders and El Capitan for oil exploration. In 1934, this land was sold to a corporation formed by Hunter and Matt Grisham and his brother Thomas, among others. It was Hunter who developed a complex water line system that allowed his ranch to receive the water it needed to operate.

In 1938, the *Dallas Morning News* ran an article about Hunter offering 1,500 acres of land as a Texas state park. When asked how he could possibly part with this land, Hunter responded, "Such natural beauty should be preserved in its primitive state for the American people. It belongs to them, even though I hold the title to the land. How can anyone consider himself owner of this magnificent land, when these mountains have been here for several million years, and I'll be lucky to be around for 70?"

Sadly, Hunter's prediction would come true, as he passed away at age fifty-five.

Before Hunter was finished, he would be the proud owner of nearly the entire Texas portion of the mountain range, which would become known as the Guadalupe Mountain Ranch. This ranch would become a testament to the Hunter family's great conservational mindset, proving their great love of the mountains as more than just landownership. Hunter shared his vision with his son, J.C. Hunter Jr., who would carry on the family legacy after his father's death in 1945.

The Guadalupe Mountain Ranch would come to include the magnificent El Capitan, McKittrick Canyon, Williams Ranch on the west side of the Guadalupes and Smith Springs (Frijole Ranch) to the east, which Hunter Sr. purchased for $5,000 in 1942. Today, Smith Springs and the Williams Ranch are still available for visitors to tour and learn about the history of the rugged mountain range.

Hunter and the Grisham-Hunter Corporation would prove to be huge supporters of turning his ranch and the surrounding land in the Guadalupe Mountains into a national park. Hunter was also a visionary in proposing a plan for a highway to connect Carlsbad, New Mexico, with El Paso, Texas, some 178 miles away. It was his hope that this beautiful land would remain pristine for future generations to enjoy.

J.C. Hunter Jr.

In a 1964 interview for *Sports Illustrated* magazine, J.C. Hunter Jr. said:

> *My dad really cared about these mountains and about preserving them in their original state. He believed they were unique in the country and that it*

> *was a privilege to protect them for the future. When he died in 1945, he had bought up about two-thirds of the land. Since then, I have bought the rest to keep it as he would have done. The canyon* [McKittrick] *has never been grazed, nor has any of the timber been cut. It looks today almost exactly as it looked in the days of the Apaches.*

Hunter Jr. had garnered respect from national figures and locals alike as a civic leader, having served as the mayor of Abilene, Texas, for six years. He was also highly involved in the family oil business and interests, one of which was his father's ranch in the Guadalupe Mountains. After his father's death in 1945, J.C. Hunter Jr. would nearly double the size of the ranch to 67,213 acres.

The National Park Service reported that in 1961, after a visit from a reconnaissance team, Hunter seriously began to consider selling his family's significant landholdings in the mountains to the National Park Service. The team made a convincing argument, stating that the land would be conserved for the enjoyment of the public.

As he became older, Hunter Jr. became more interested in selling off some of his landholdings, so he contacted Millerman and Millerman Realty to start the process. Realtor Glenn Biggs was working for the firm at the time and was given the task of promoting the sale of the ranch. At first, the property was offered as a commercial ranching site. All three groups that considered buying the property for commercial interests sent back negative feedback. This turn of events set into motion a huge push to establish Guadalupe Mountains National Park, with Biggs suggesting the idea of the park to Secretary of the Interior Stewart Udall.

As a member of the United States Highway 180 Association, Biggs was in contact with many people who shared his vision and were enthusiastic about the formation of a national park. This cause became a passion for Biggs, who would host tours of the mountains for dignitaries. On a wall at the Guadalupe Mountains National Park Visitors' Center, there is a plaque from the United States Highway 180 Association that reads:

> *The United States Highway 180 Association salutes the inspiring leadership and dedication of the "committee of five" for their untiring efforts in the development and promotion of the Guadalupe Mountains National Park. Dedicated to: Glenn Biggs—Abilene, Texas; Claude Brown—McCamey, Texas; William Adair Gossett—Carlsbad, New Mexico; John Ben Shepperd—Odessa, Texas; and Louis M. Whitlock—Carlsbad, New Mexico.*

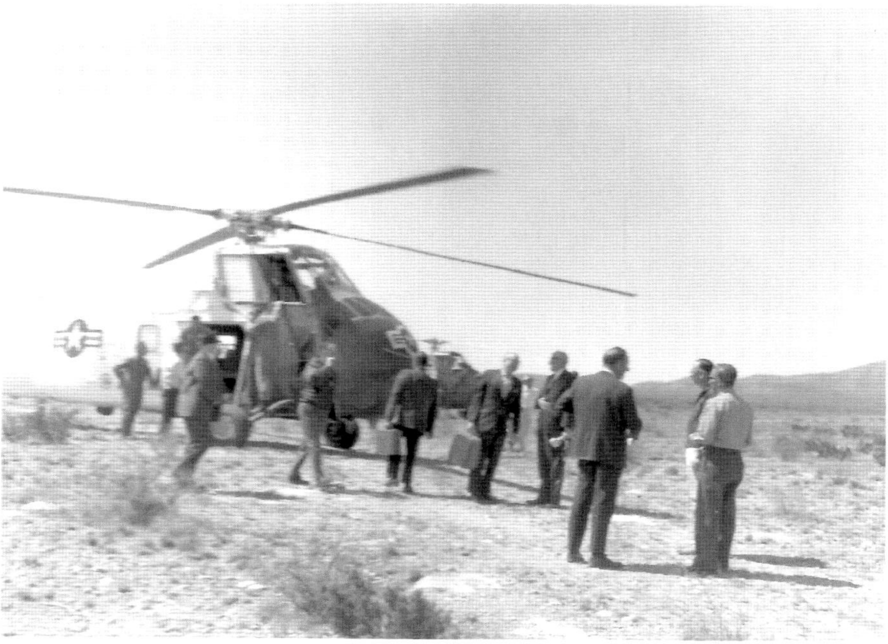

A helicopter filled with dignitaries from the U.S. Senate Subcommittee on National Parks lands on Wallace Pratt's private airstrip at the mouth of McKittrick Canyon. *Courtesy Guadalupe Mountains National Park.*

A park proposal was sent to Governor Connally in September 1963, but due to President Kennedy's assassination and Governor Connally's long recovery, it was not to be. New president Lyndon B. Johnson would then champion the cause. The turning point of the negotiations came when Stewart Udall was given a helicopter tour of the mountains, during which he was heard to say the words "wonderful" and "spectacular" many times. He also noted that the Guadalupe Mountains were a "natural wonder of Texas."

In 1966, Hunter Jr. sold his beloved ranch to the National Park Service for $1.5 million after a series of agreements and years of negotiations. Originally, the U.S. government wanted to purchase small parcels of the land, an idea Hunter originally refused but ultimately agreed to by selling only the least-desirable plots. By February 1968, Hunter had deeded 14,007.06 acres of his land to the government for a total of $280,000. In 1969, he conveyed an additional 9,773.25 acres for $205,000. The final 48,290.55 acres was deeded in November 1969 for $1,015,000 for a grand total of $1.5 million. This deal also brought the ire of those who said Hunter should have donated

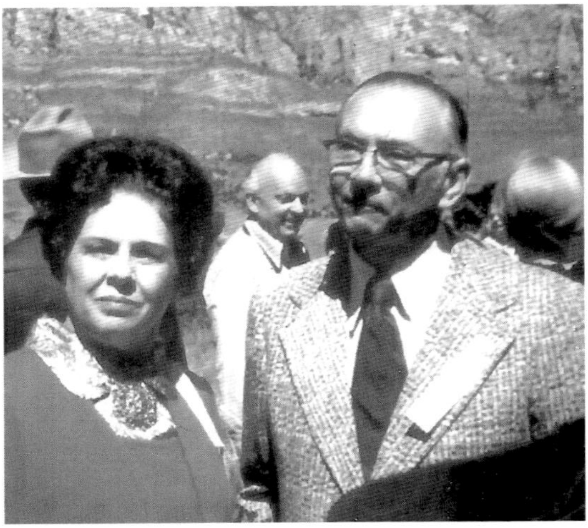

J.C. Hunter Jr. and his wife, Mary, at the dedication ceremony of the Guadalupe Mountains in 1972. *Courtesy Guadalupe Mountains National Park.*

his land like his neighbor, Wallace Pratt. Undaunted, Hunter knew that this sale was best for his family and for the preservation of McKittrick Canyon as well.

Wallace E. Pratt

Born in Kansas, Wallace E. Pratt was the sixth child of ten in the household. For Pratt, opportunities were as low as the family's income. But he worked hard and put himself through college, completing his master's degree in 1909. After college, Pratt went to work for the Division of Mines in the Philippine Islands. He was once quoted as saying, "I had to go halfway around the world to get a job." Promoted to chief, Pratt returned to the United States in 1915 and accepted a position with the Texas Company in Mexico. During strife, Pratt and his co-workers were thrown into a Mexican jail and were later rescued by American gunboats.

Pratt would eventually become one of the largest supporters of McKittrick Canyon—but he was not always of that mindset. As a geologist for Humble Oil, he was originally sent to the area to scout for natural gas spots and oil deposits in the Pecos Valley region. Early into his exploration of the area, he was "more interested in the rocks than the men," according to an interview about the origin of the canyon's name. But when Pratt was introduced to the Guadalupe Mountains by Culberson County judge Robert Drane, he

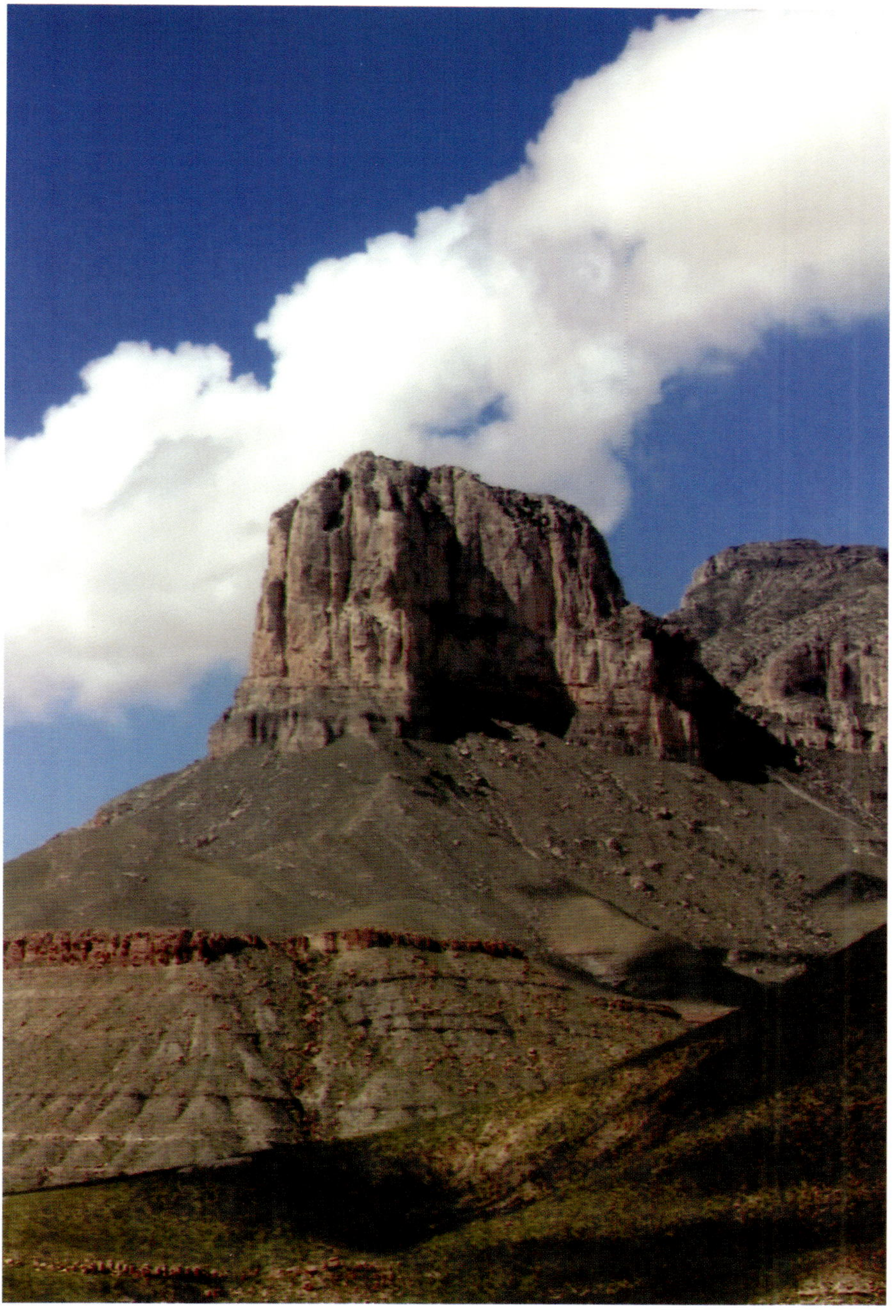

El Capitan (also Signal Peak or, as it was called by the Spanish Conquistadors, Cathedral Mountain) rises proudly over the Capitan Reef, providing an unmistakable landmark for all those who travel in the Guadalupe Mountains area. *Author's collection.*

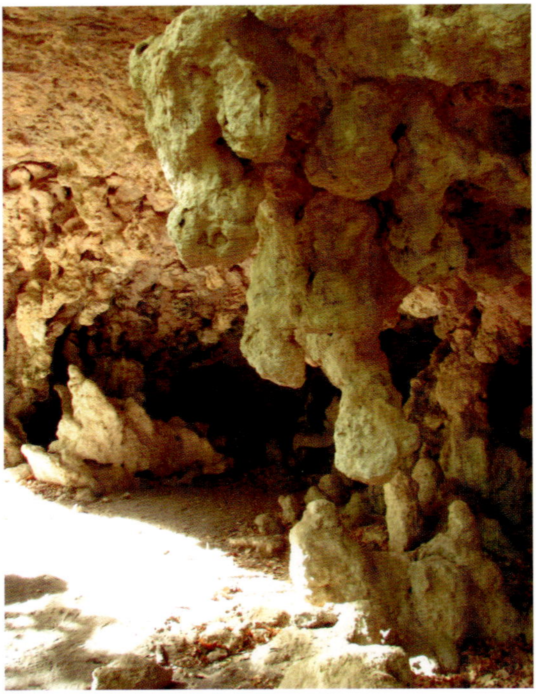

On the way to Hunter's Lodge, hikers will encounter a naturally formed grotto. This limestone formation was created much like the nearby Carlsbad Caverns—one drop of water at a time. *Author's collection.*

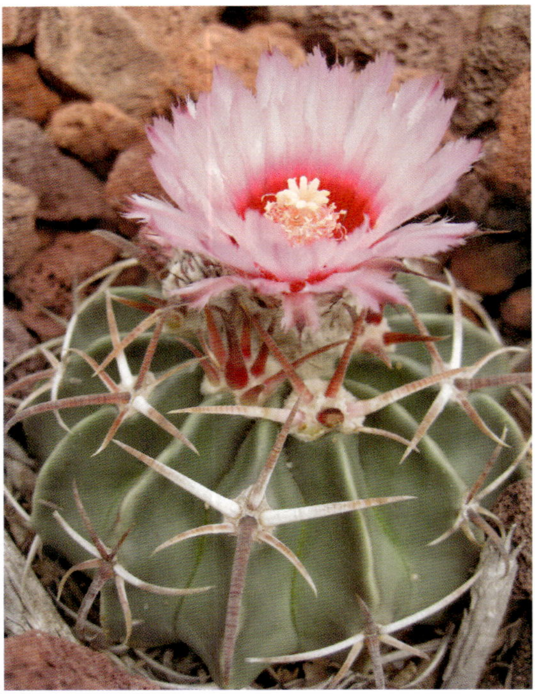

Many species of cacti survive in the canyon environment. The *Echinocactus horizonthalonius*, commonly known as horse crippler, is one of the more dramatic with its thick, curved spines. *Courtesy Flickr user Aka Hige.*

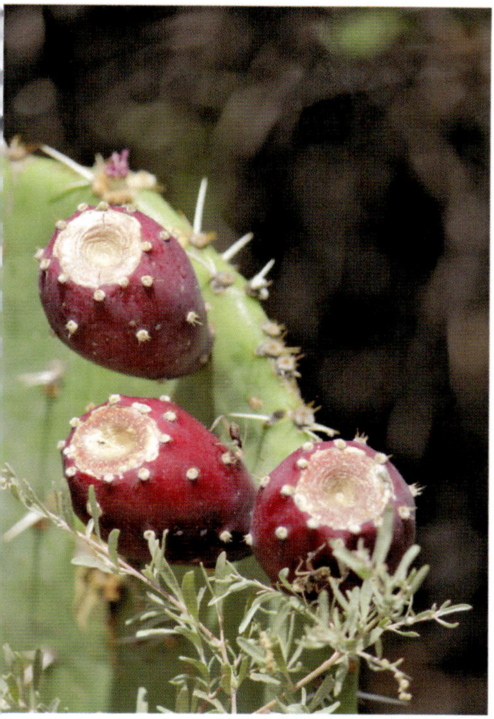

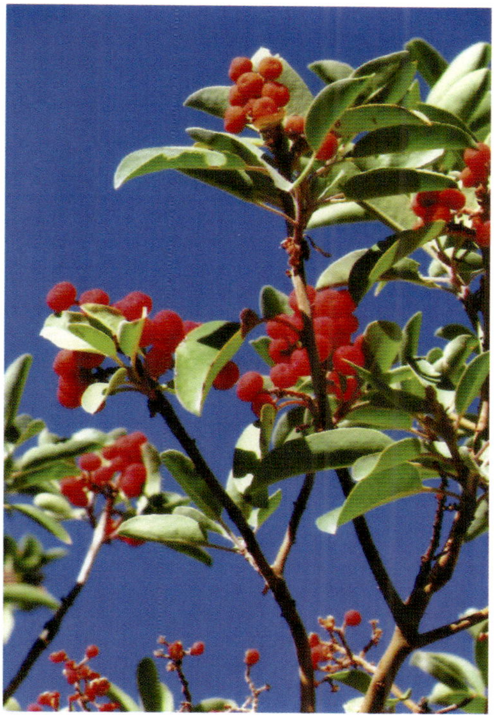

Above, left: Native Americans used the fruit of the prickly pear cactus for sweeteners, and early settlers made tasty jams and jellies from the plentiful plant. *Author's collection.*

Above, right: Called *manzanita* (little apples) by locals, the berries of the Texas madrone tree are bright red and can be made into jelly. *Author's collection.*

Right: The approach to Pratt's Stone Cabin is heralded by stone walls and spires, giving it a feeling of the Northeast. *Author's collection.*

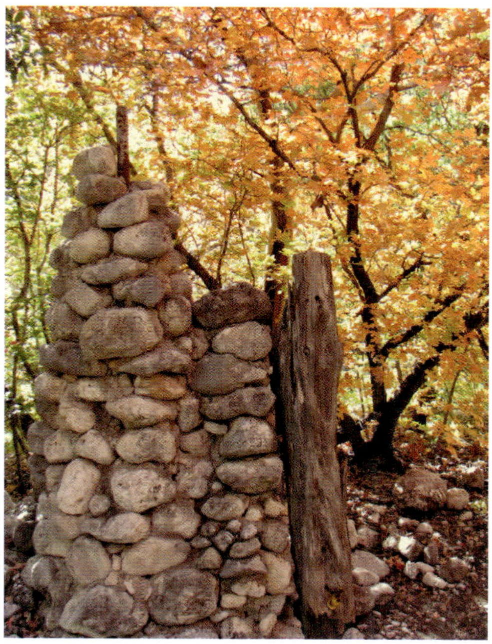

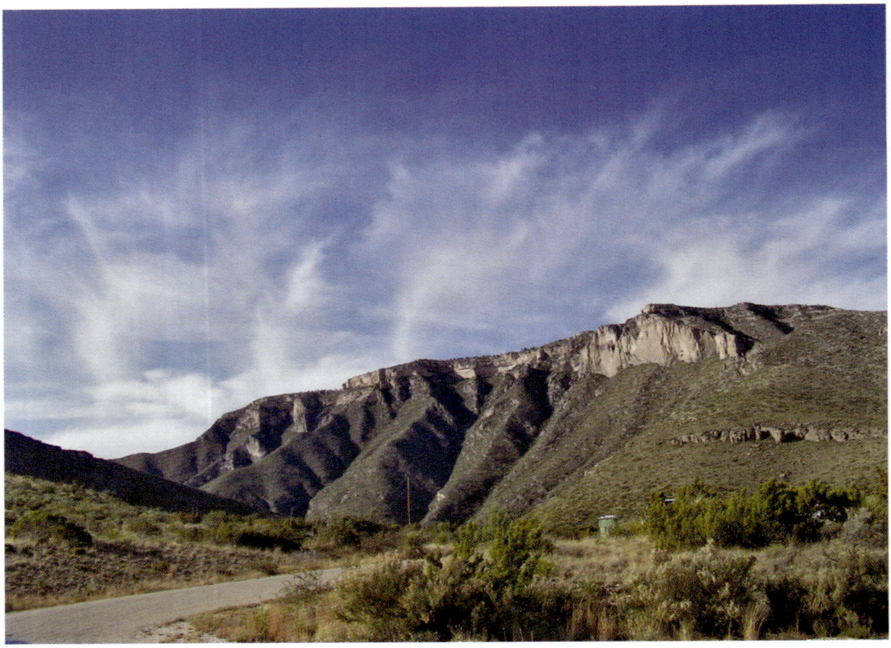

The majestic McKittrick Canyon Rim welcomes all who visit this unique landform. *Author's collection.*

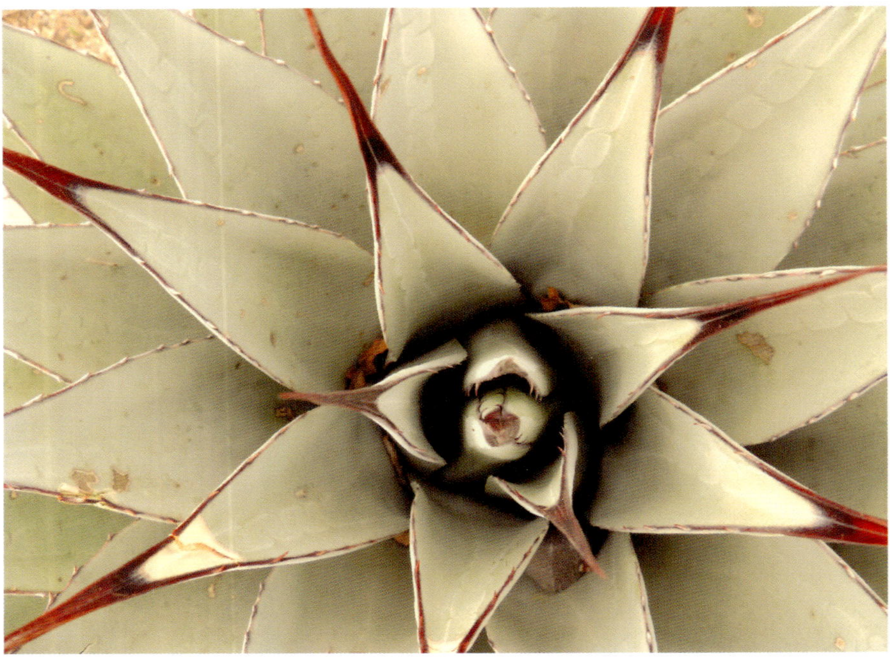

Right: Limestone cliffs loom two thousand feet over the canyon floor as ancient centennials watching over the beauty below. *Author's collection.*

Opposite, bottom: Lechuguilla, a cousin to the agave, is a formable presence in McKittrick Canyon. The extremely sharp points of the plant's petals contain a powerful poison that can incapacitate both animal and human. *Courtesy Olivia Danielle Ruiz via Wikimedia Commons.*

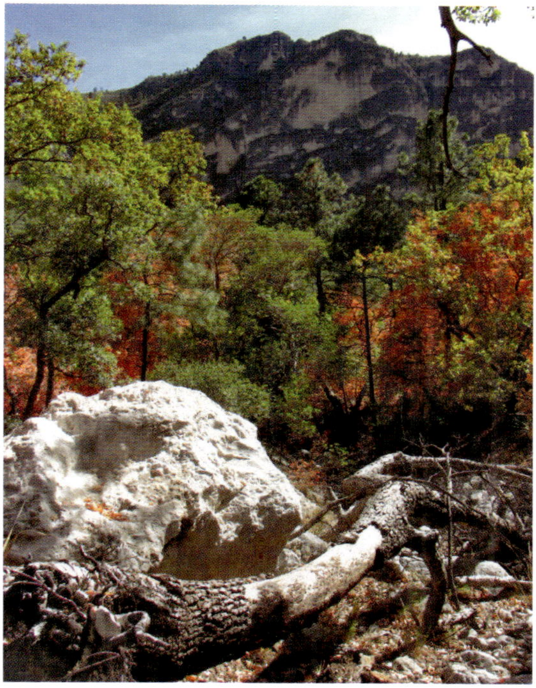

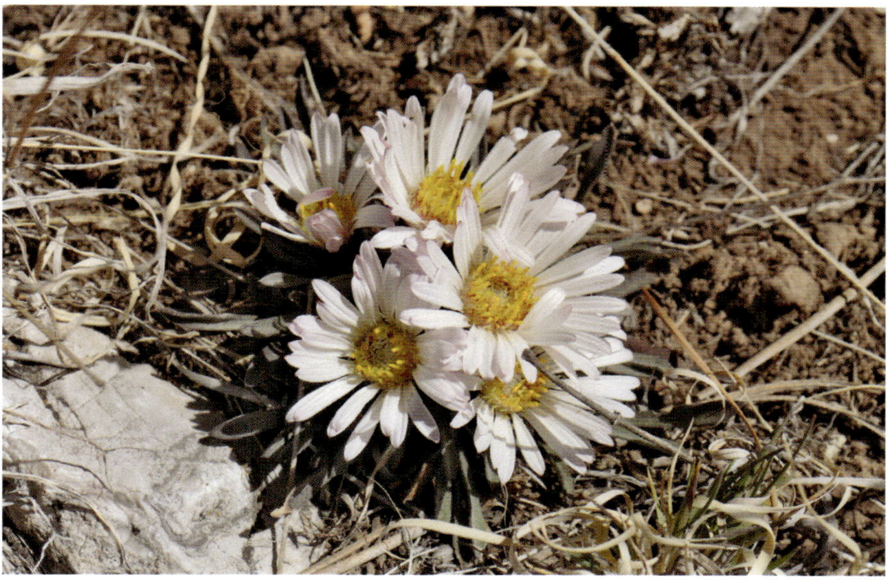

Wildflowers such as these daisies blanket the canyon floor after a spring rain, bringing a different array of colors than what McKittrick Canyon is generally known for. *Wikimedia Commons.*

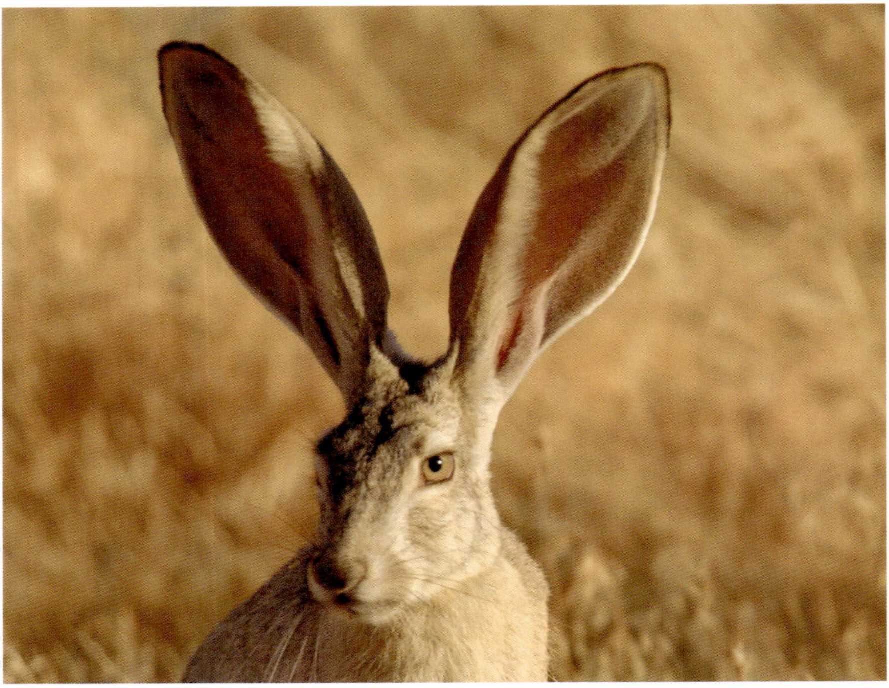

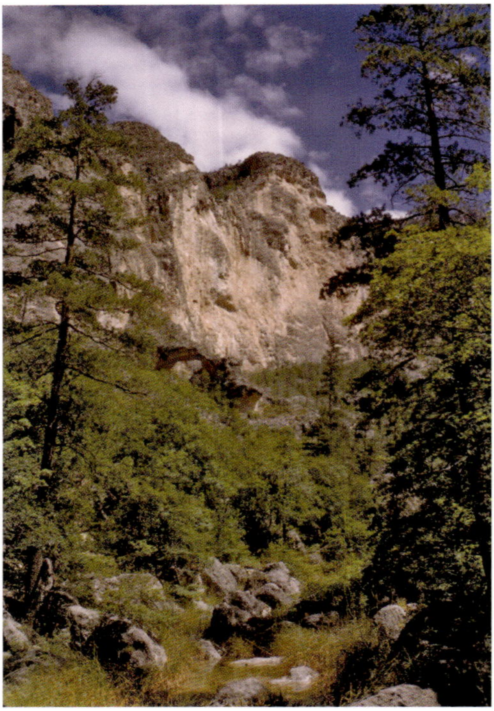

Above: Black-tailed jackrabbits (*Lepus californicus*) make a meal of the many types of grasses and shrubs that populate the canyon. Once rare during periods of drought, the jackrabbit is once again showing up in the canyon. *Courtesy Scott Rheam, U.S. Fish and Wildlife Service.*

Left: The limestone walls behind the Stone Cabin are said to be one of the best places on earth to study how the Capitan Reef was formed. *Courtesy National Park Service Digital Image Archives.*

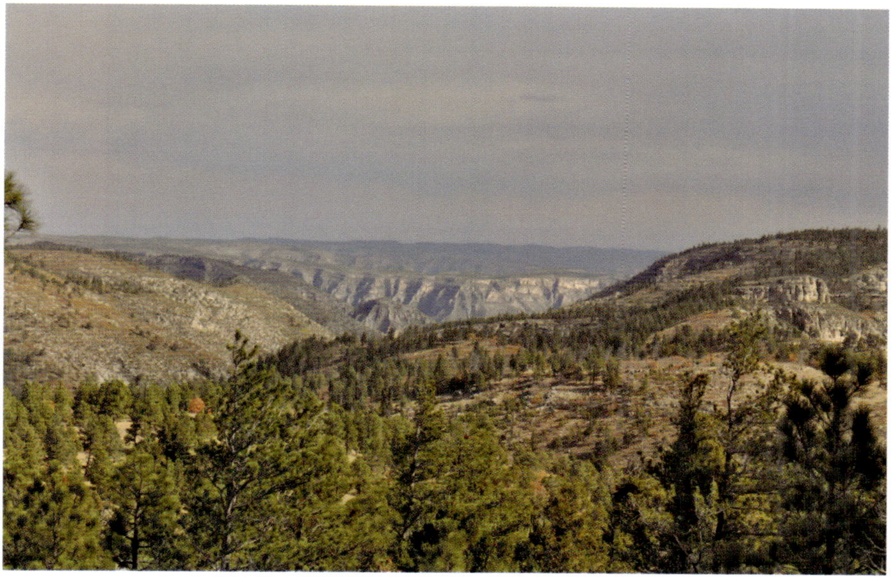

Above: A view of McKittrick Ridge from Hunter's Peak. *Wikimedia Commons*.

Right: A fallen oak provides a natural bridge into a hidden glen along the trail to Hunter's Lodge. *Author's collection*.

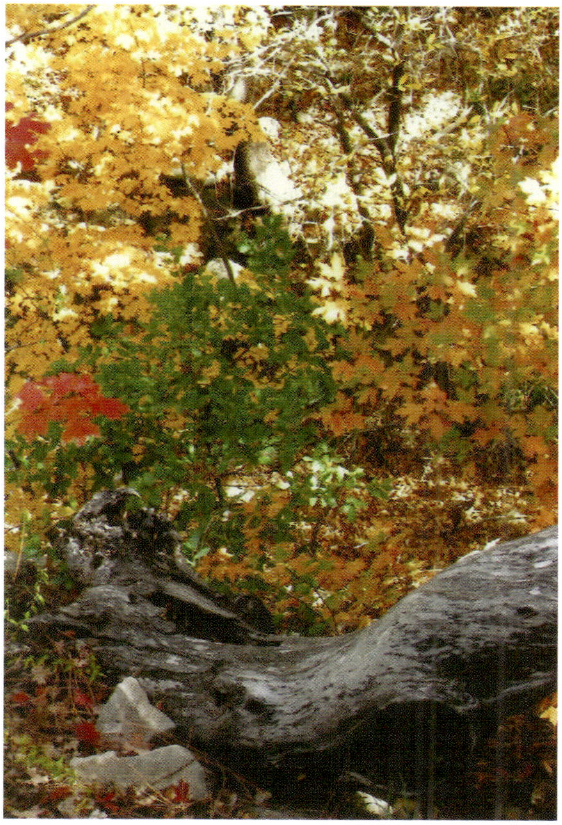

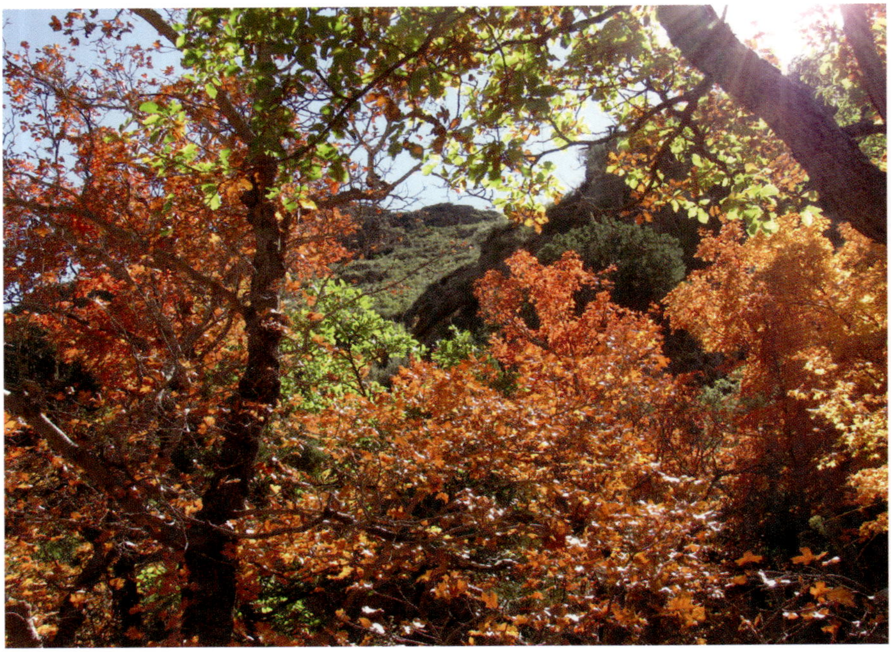

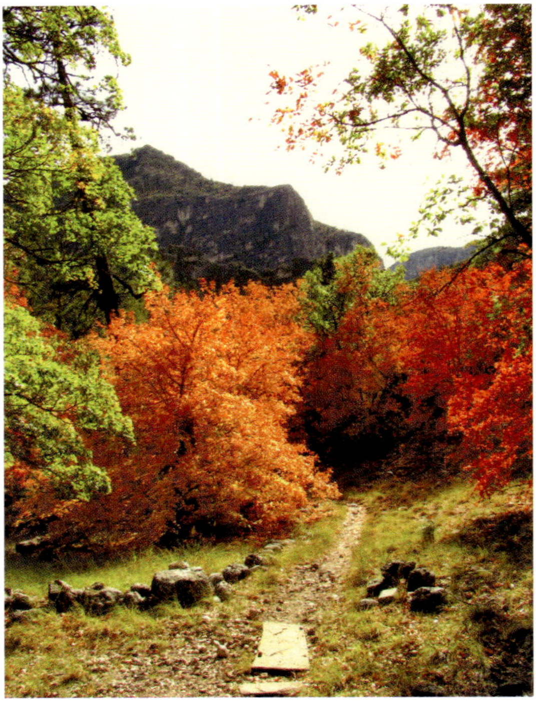

Above: The sun shines through the festive fall foliage at McKittrick Canyon, giving a glimpse of why thousands of people visit the canyon each year. *Author's collection*.

Left: A stone path leads hikers deeper into McKittrick Canyon's beauty. *Author's collection*.

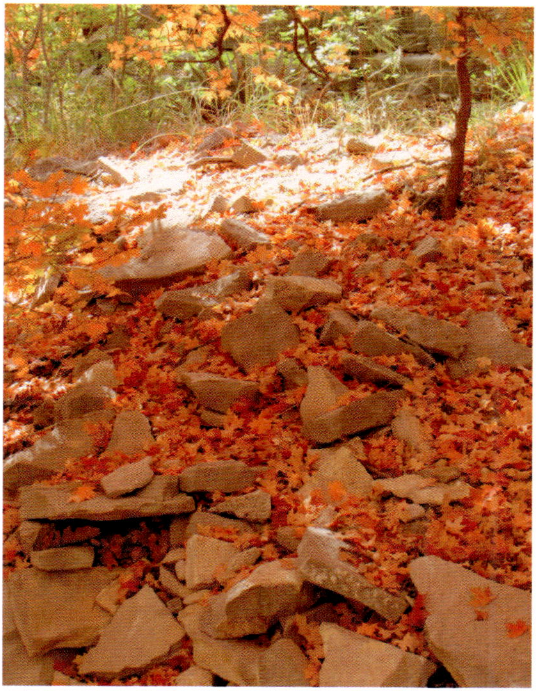

The limestone quarry in McKittrick Canyon from which building stones were taken to construct the Stone Cabin. *Author's collection.*

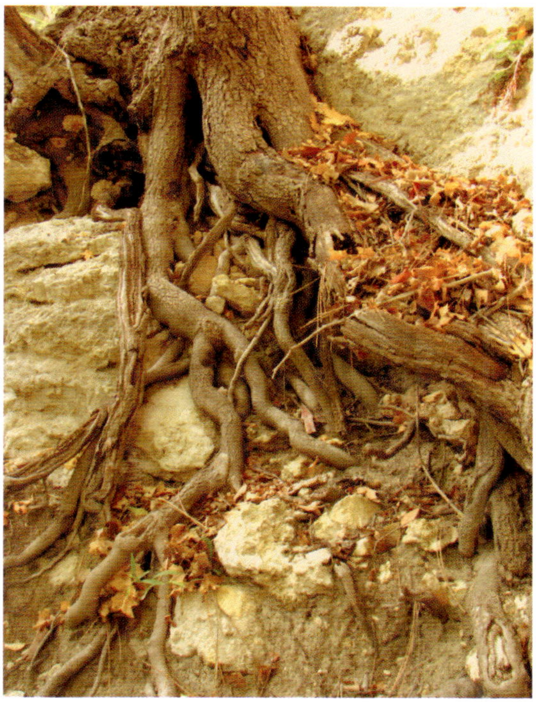

The exposed, twisted roots of an oak tree cling to the limestone layers. *Author's collection.*

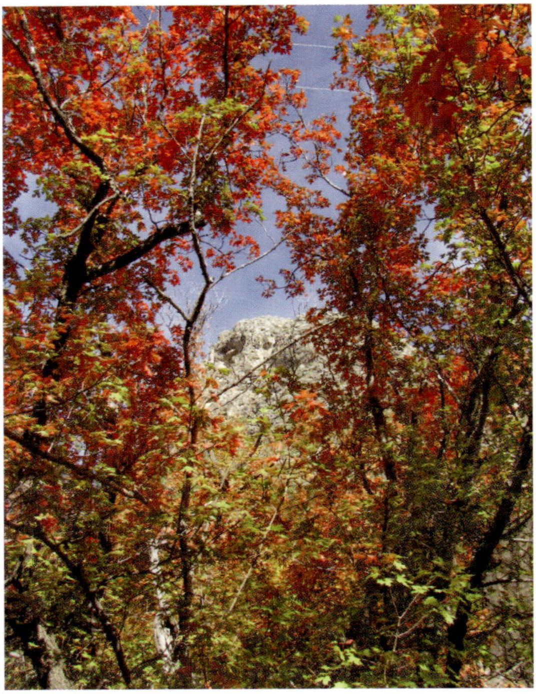

Bright foliage is what McKittrick Canyon is best known for. Each year presents new and wonderful vistas to enjoy. *Author's collection.*

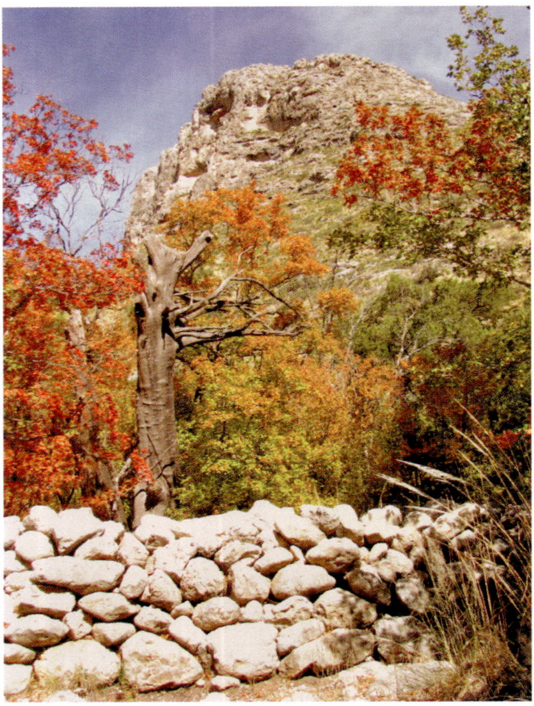

Artfully constructed stone walls fence in the main yard of Pratt's Stone Cabin, providing a home for many species of rodents, birds and small animals. *Author's collection.*

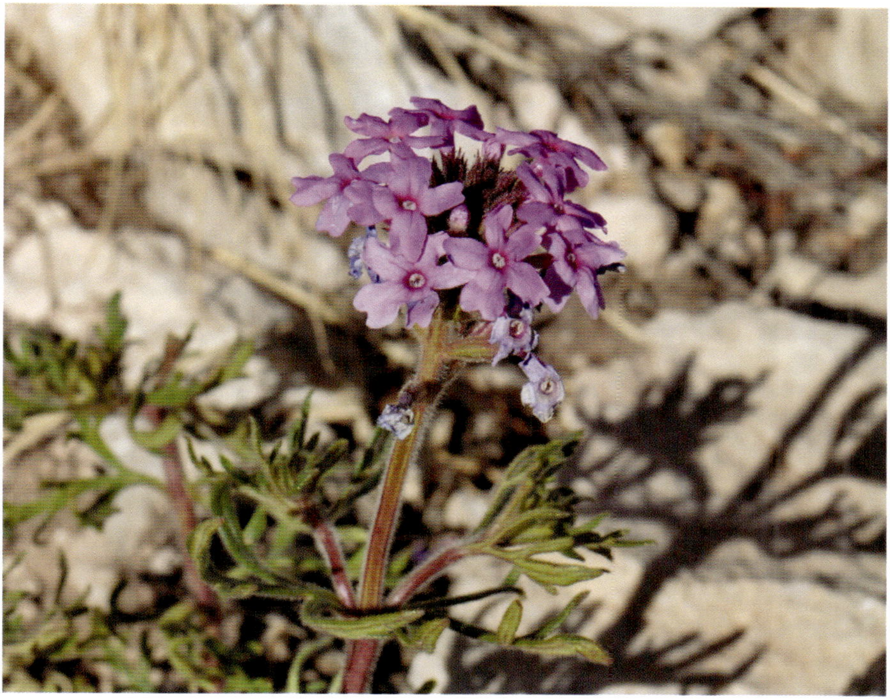

Above: Delicate purple wildflowers add even more beauty to the canyon. *Wikimedia Commons*.

Right: It's easy to see why McKittrick Canyon was described as the "most beautiful spot in Texas." *Author's collection*.

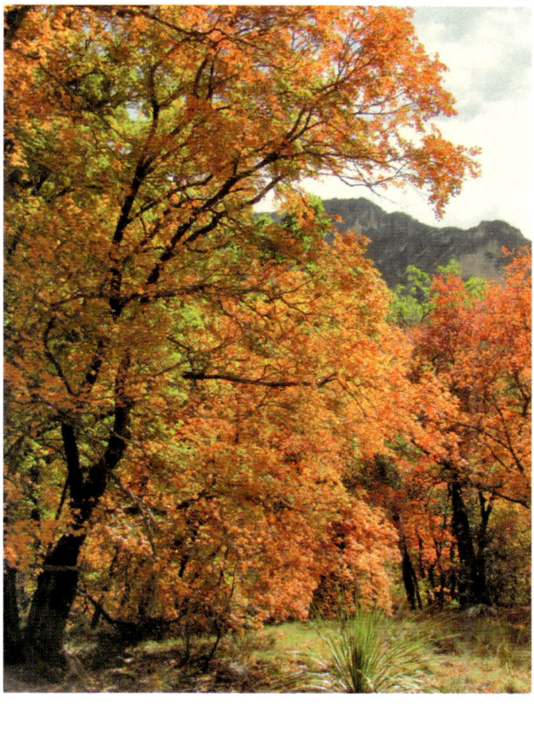

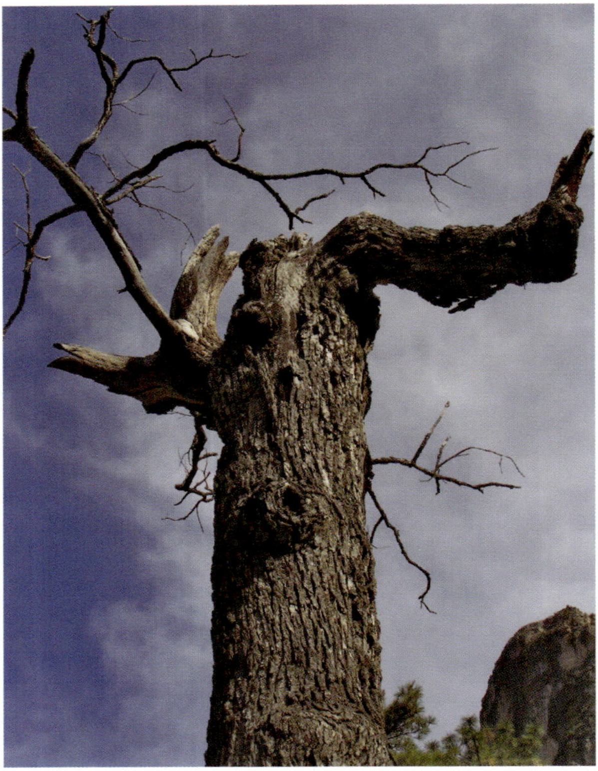

Left: The skeleton of an alligator juniper reaches its craggy branches into the mountain air. *Author's collection.*

Below and opposite, top: The cholla cactus is a nemesis of humans and animals alike, as it has a tendency to reach out and grab anything that crosses its path. *Courtesy Rennett Stowe via Flickr.*

Opposite, bottom: Vibrant red blooms of the claret cup cactus add even more color to an already stunning landscape. *Author's collection.*

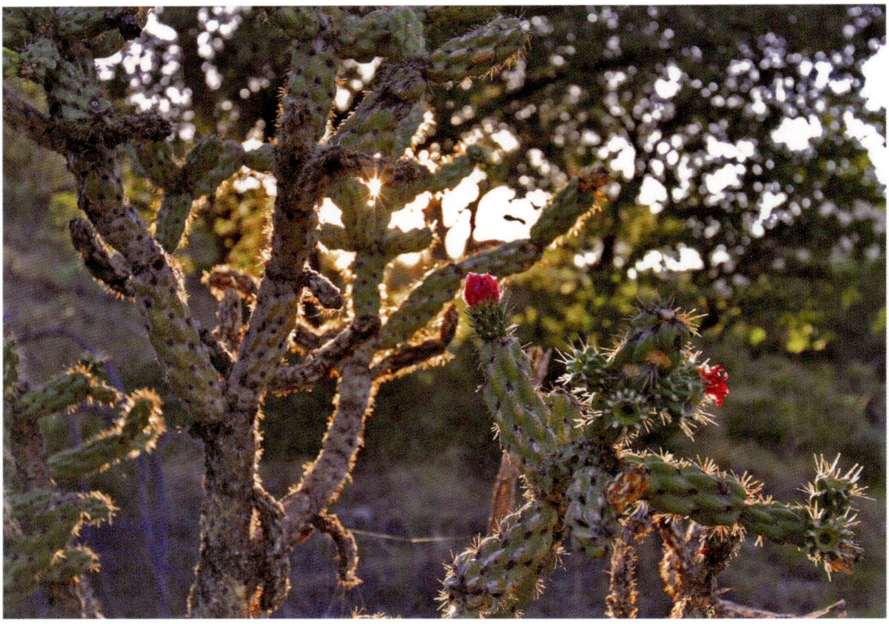

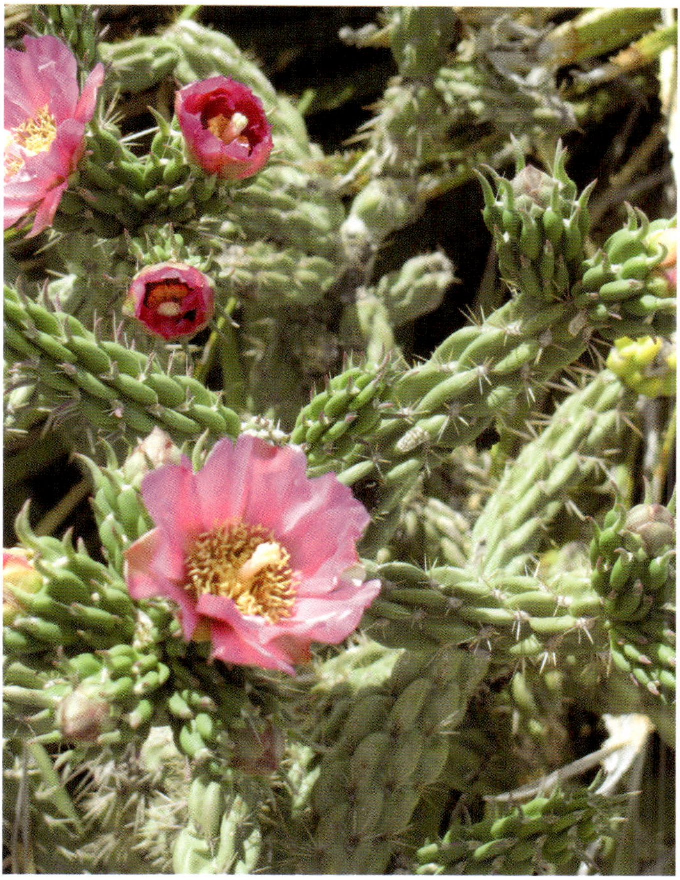

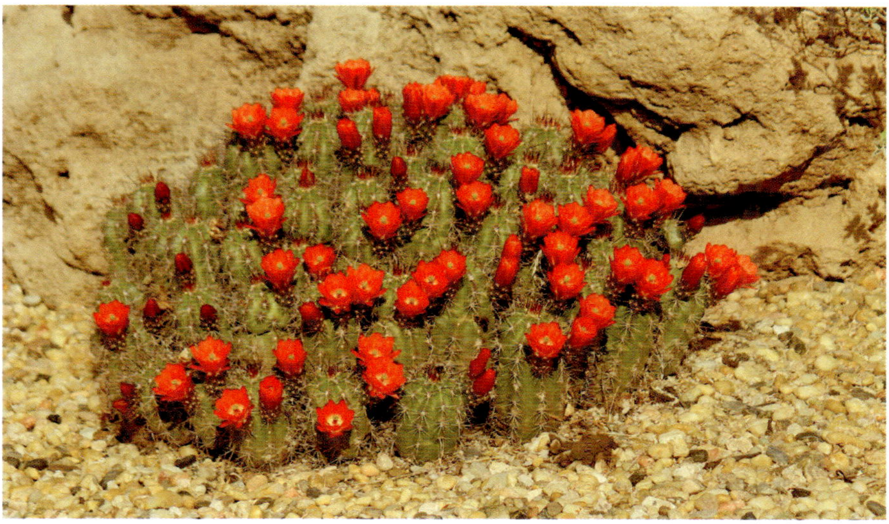

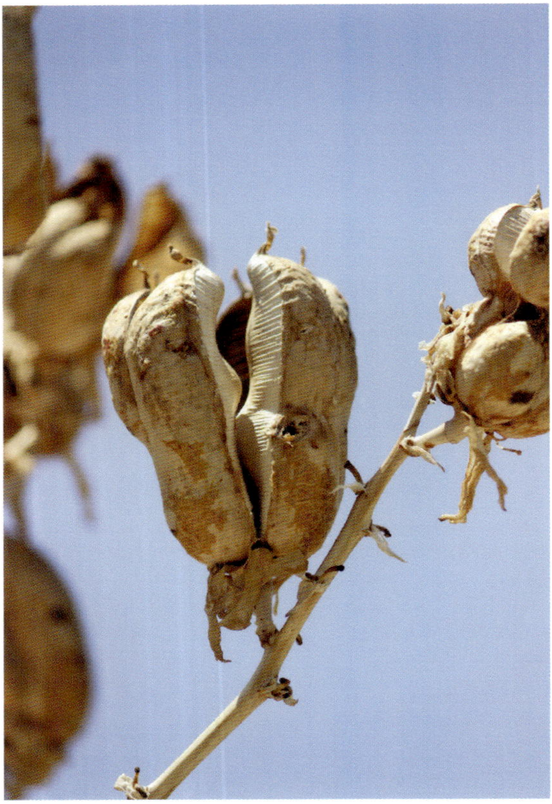

Left: Yuccas depend on the yucca moth for pollination. Likewise, the moth uses the yuccas as a food source. Hundreds of seeds are housed in the yucca pods and are ready for collection when they turn black. *Author's collection.*

Below: Blooming in hues of yellows, reds and peaches, the prickly pear blossom is a beautiful crown on a plant that is native to North America and in some regions considered a noxious weed. *Author's collection.*

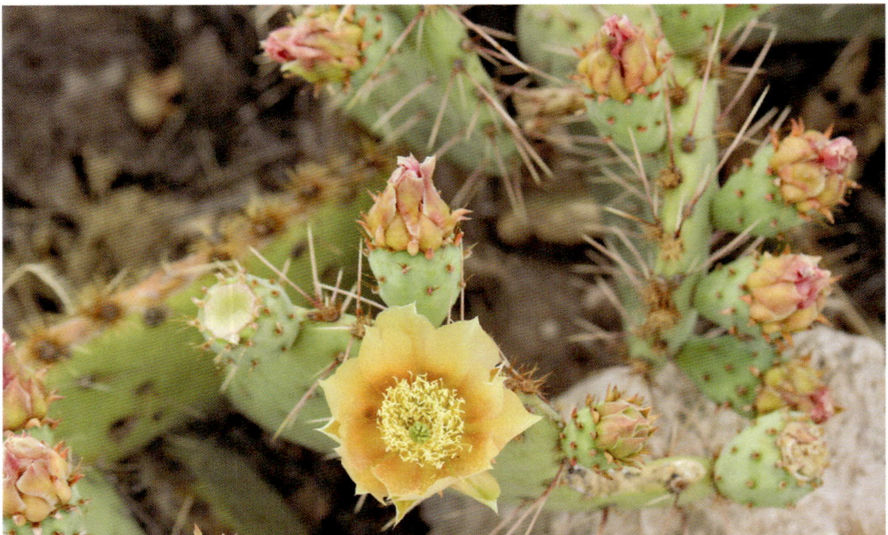

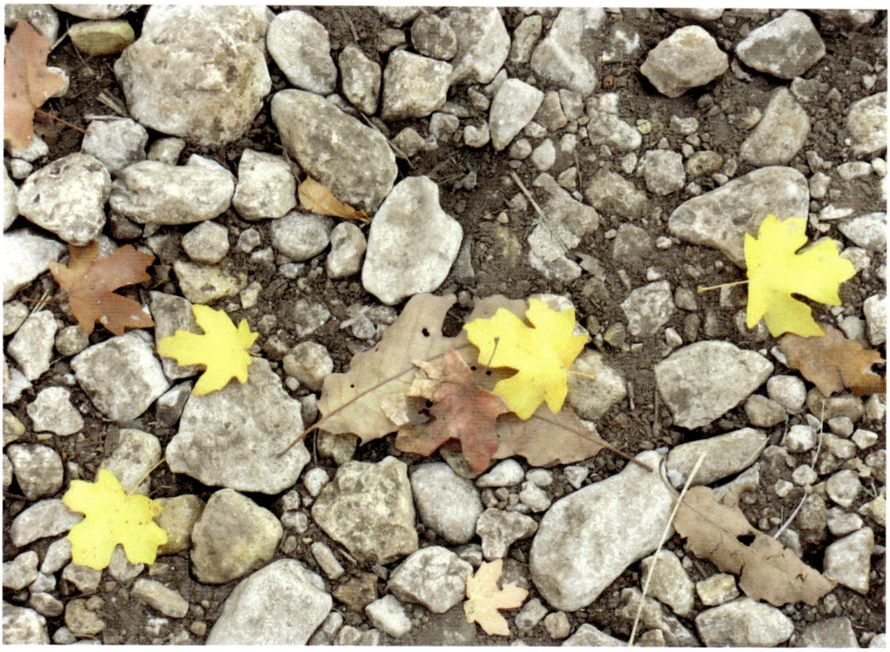

Above: Mother Nature shows her artistic side in the placement of these fall leaves. *Author's collection*.

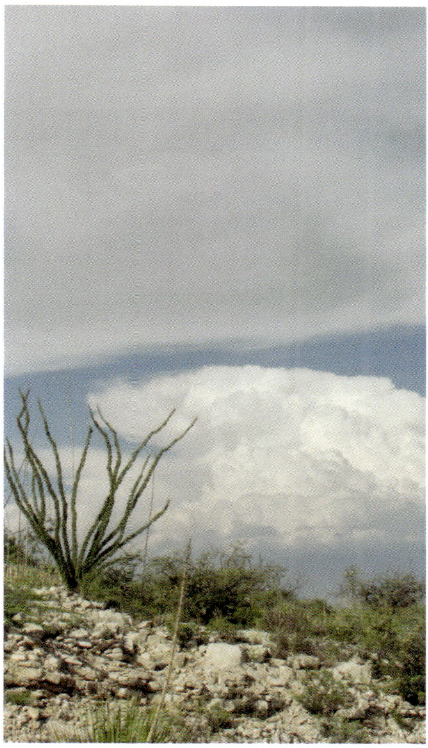

Right: The ocotillo, also called a candlewood, is not actually a true cactus. Found throughout the Southwest, the spiny plant was used by Native Americans to slow the bleeding on fresh wounds. *Author's collection*.

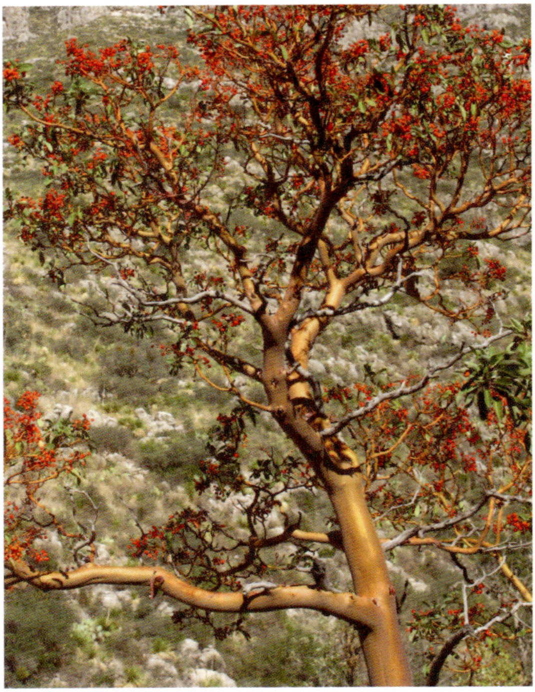

Rare and gorgeous, the Texas madrone is found only in certain parts of New Mexico and Texas that are above three thousand feet in elevation. *Author's collection.*

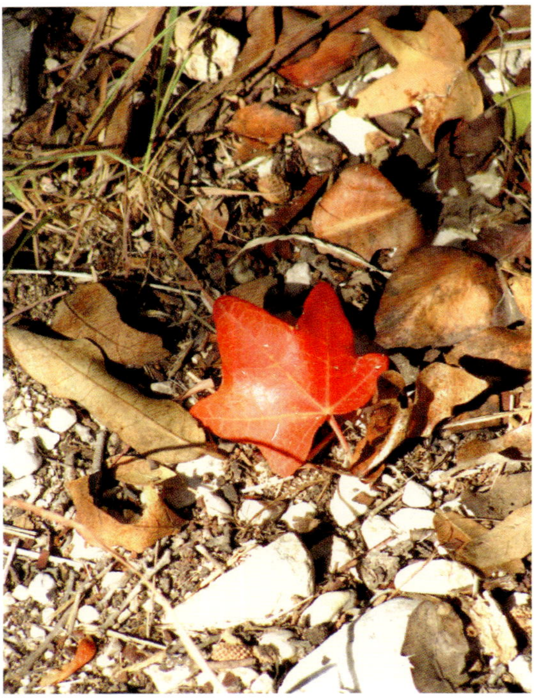

Maple and oak leaves line the floor of McKittrick Canyon and provide a habitat for the tiniest dwellers of its unique ecosystem. *Author's collection.*

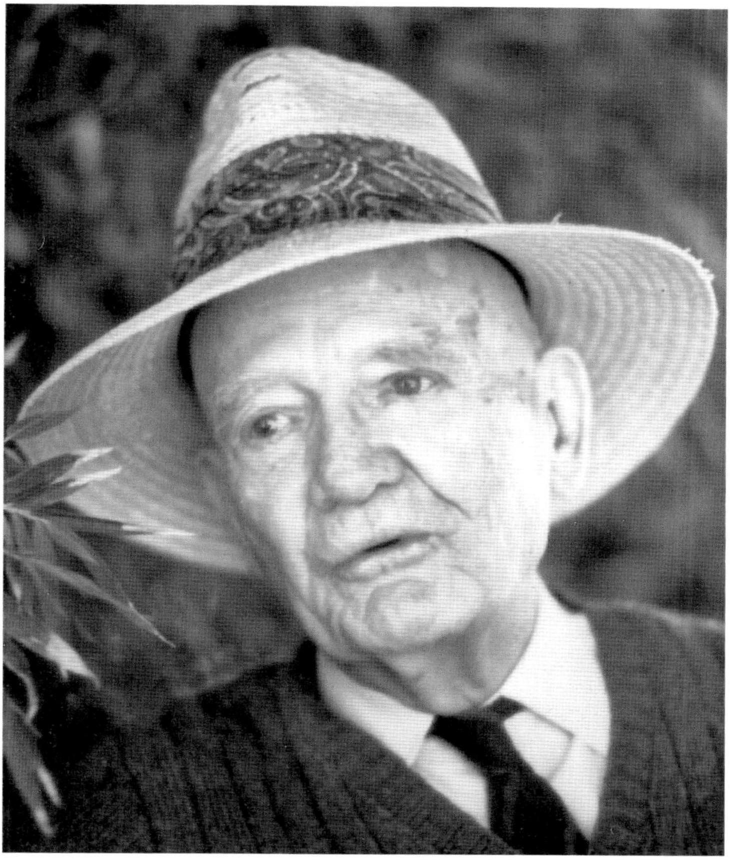

A portrait of Wallace E. Pratt, who generously donated his ranch to the National Park Service for the great enjoyment of others. *Courtesy Guadalupe Mountains National Park.*

immediately recognized their value from both a geologic standpoint and as a place of residence. After a grueling one-hundred-mile trip on rough roads in a Model-T Ford, Pratt was introduced to a land so beautiful that he immediately fell in love.

It would also be Wallace Pratt who would negotiate the first oil lease on the now-825,000-acre King Ranch in Kingsville, Texas, giving the ranch some much-needed capital after the Second World War.

In 1921, over seventy thousand acres of the Guadalupe Mountains, including McKittrick Canyon, came up for sale. The property, which was listed for $1.5 million (close to $10 million in today's economy), was advertised as having an abundant spring, numerous pipelines and wells and twenty-three thousand acres of oil leases. Also included were a good portion of the mineral rights, as well as hunting and fishing rights. When the realtor offered to show the land to Pratt, he prefaced it by saying, "I want to show you the most beautiful spot in Texas"—a phrase Pratt would use repeatedly to describe his beautiful canyon.

After purchasing the land, Pratt decided to build a retirement home in the canyon for him and his first wife, Pearl. Unfortunately, Pearl was lost in the Gulf of Mexico after she went for a swim and tragically never returned. Pratt, now a widower, started a consulting business in Carlsbad, New Mexico, and moved to Texas in 1949. He would later travel by private airplane from Texas to New Mexico with his second wife, Iris Calderhead. After receiving his pilot's license at age forty-eight, Pratt had a landing strip built close to the mouth of McKittrick Canyon for his frequent trips. He reluctantly gave up flying at the age of seventy-six.

Whenever Pratt, always the geologist and oilman, flew over a promising oil-producing formation, he would call it in to the company. These tips were affectionately known as "hot potatoes" at the company. Of his profession as a geologist, Pratt often remarked, "It has been my marvelous good fortune that my avocation has been my vocation." Humble about his accolades, Pratt, who was widely touted as a visionary in the oil and gas industry, as well as a world-class geologist, would also say, "I was lucky—the time just happened to be ripe for someone with my bag of tricks to come down the pike."

Immensely concerned with the ecology of the Guadalupe Mountains, Pratt deeded his beloved McKittrick Canyon to the National Park Service in 1961 with a firm stipulation that Guadalupe Mountains National Park be established. The fulfillment of this stipulation would not occur until 1972, at which time the Pratts were living in Tucson due to Iris's failing health. Unfortunately, she would die shortly afterward. At Iris's request, her ashes were scattered over McKittrick Canyon.

Pratt's ranch is described as a "masterpiece of conservation and preservation" by the rangers of the Guadalupe Mountains National Park.

Wallace Pratt was a fixture at any and all Guadalupe Mountains National Park events and would tirelessly promote his favorite place on earth well into his late eighties, often giving long speeches about the history and geology of the region that gave him such pleasure.

By 1966, Pratt had married for the third time to Suzanne d'Autremont, who knew Iris and survived him along with his three children after his death on Christmas Day 1981 at the age of ninety-six. A prolific letter writer,

Pratt is said to have been up all night on Christmas Eve dictating letters. One of his most endearing habits was to include his wife in all of his correspondences—it was always "we," never "I."

When asked about his reasons for donating his 5,632 acres of McKittrick Canyon to the National Park Service, Pratt replied:

> *We served our selfish purpose. We gave them our home and the mountains, and we got the preservation of a barrier reef that is unique in the western hemisphere. My intent in it was aesthetic, not professional; I had been told simply that it was the most beautiful spot in Texas. So I drove a hundred miles in an old Model T to see for myself…We suddenly realized we couldn't take care of ourselves anymore. We were old. And we thought, "My God, what's going to become of this?" We thought someone ought to take care of this wonderful barrier reef, protect it from the litter of the sightseers and the tourists. I have never been conscious of being generous; it was a way to preserve the museum that the barrier reef is.*

As per his final request, the National Park Service allowed the Pratt family to scatter the ashes of Wallace Pratt over his beloved canyon so he may forever be a part of the most beautiful spot in Texas.

Noel Kincaid

A book about McKittrick Canyon would not be complete without including Noel Kincaid. In 1936, eighteen-year-old Kincaid went to work for Judge J.C. Hunter Sr., who hired him on the spot. Unlike the other workers on the ranch, who were paid three dollars per month, Hunter insisted in paying Kincaid with four Angora goats. By 1942, Kincaid was able to buy half interest in the five-thousand-plus herd of goats at a time when Angora hair was being shipped to many places.

Although Kincaid was frustrated by his form of payment, he would work permanently for the Hunter Ranch for the next thirty years (1942–72) for both generations of landowners. They would eventually begin paying him a wage instead of in livestock. Despite his initial frustration, Kincaid reported that both Hunter men were good to work for and that he thoroughly enjoyed his job. And how could he not? To have the Guadalupe Mountains wilderness as your office would be a dream job.

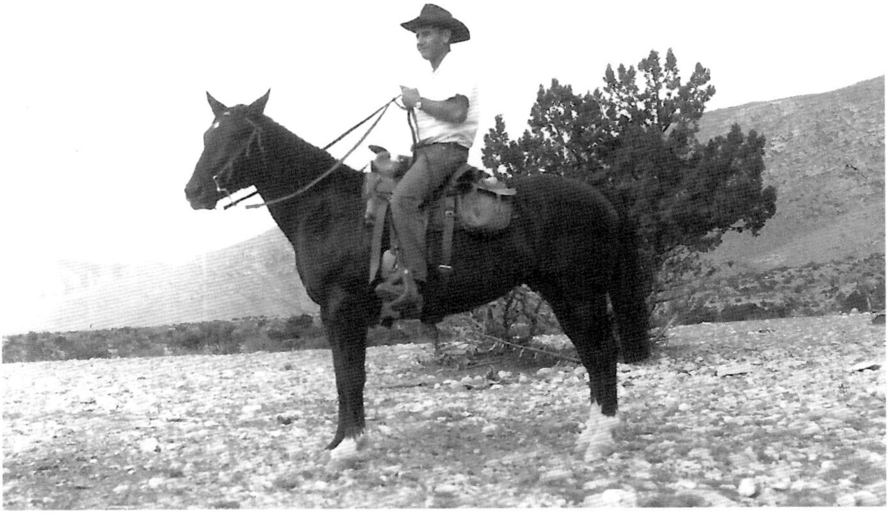

Noel Kincaid, shown here on Ranger Reisch's horse Chongo, was the backbone of the Hunter Ranch and dedicated his life to the mountains he loved. *Courtesy Guadalupe Mountains National Park.*

Noel Kincaid's father, Jack, had settled the Dog Canyon area in 1912, according to National Park Service records. Noel Kincaid would live there until 1947, when the Hunters moved him and his wife, Lucille (daughter of longtime Guadalupe Mountains rancher Scibey Cox), into the Frijole Ranch house.

An expert trail guide, Kincaid often took dignitaries and lay people alike into the backcountry of his Guadalupes. Robert Tolbert commented numerous times in his *Dallas Morning News* column about one of Kincaid's greatest skills: making biscuits. While conducting the tours by horseback, Kincaid would direct the groups to Hunter's Lodge, where they would stay the night. Being the ultimate trail guide, Kincaid would cook meals for the travelers, receiving rave reviews.

Kincaid was known for his dry sense of humor and ability to prank the "city slickers" who came to the mountains for tours. The mules that Kincaid used for the tours had distinct personalities, some not always agreeable. If Noel decided you were in need of a lesson or attitude adjustment, he placed you on a mule that would deliver that lesson in the best means possible.

Noel served as a Culberson County justice of the peace for sixteen years (1955–71) and was a member of the American Mohair Council for fifteen years and the American Quarter Horse Association for twenty-five years.

In 1958, Noel was responsible for taking the materials needed to create the Guadalupe Peak Monument, commissioned by American Airlines to commemorate the 100th anniversary of the overland mail service, when the original plan of using a helicopter was thwarted by high winds. It took him two dozen trips with a string of mules to get all the supplies and equipment to the top of the 8,751-foot peak, which had no established trails at the time. This monument is a goal for hikers both young and old and offers one of the most spectacular views in the entire park system. The names written into a logbook tucked safely into a metal container at the top attest to the immense attraction of the peak. The Guadalupe Mountains National Park has all the copies carefully archived in its library.

After several tragic plane crashes in the Guadalupes (two military and several civilian), Noel was given the grim task of using his pack team for the removal of the bodies. Remnants of these crashes still exist on the mountainside.

Chief Justice William O. Douglas mentioned Noel in his book *Farewell to Texas*: "Noel Kincaid, who is not only a good ranch foreman and justice of the peace, but also the best architect of hot biscuits I knew, spoke up to say, 'No road should ever get beyond this Lodge [Hunter's].'" Kincaid knew the treasure of McKittrick Canyon and worked against the commercialization of the land.

Once his beloved land became a national park, Kincaid left the area and moved to Alpine, Texas, where he managed a twenty-seven-thousand-acre ranch. He would eventually move back to Carlsbad, where he worked with the Carlsbad Irrigation District until the age of seventy-five.

Noel Kincaid was described as "a down-to-earth rancher who took no guff." He did not see the prestige; he saw the person. His life was marked with great triumphs and, closer to the end, great tragedies. But through it all, he was in control and did things his own way.

Glenn Biggs

An instrumental player in the development of the beautiful Guadalupe Mountains becoming a national park, Glenn Biggs worked tirelessly as a real estate agent and economic developer for J.C. Hunter Jr. He promoted the seventy-eight-thousand-plus-acre ranch for purchase by the Department of the Interior, and it was ultimately relinquished to his control.

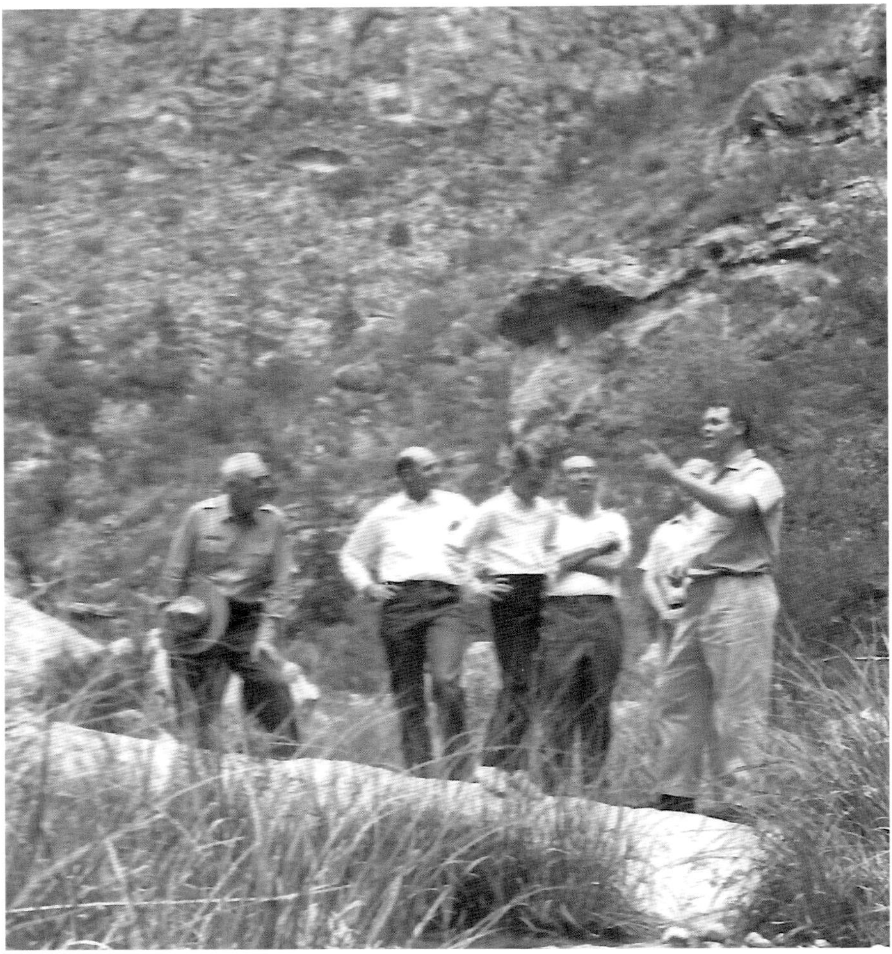

In 1964, government representatives toured McKittrick Canyon at the request of one of its largest supporters, Glenn Biggs. Featured in South McKittrick Canyon are, from left to right, Superintendent During, New Mexico state representative Tom Morris, his son Tommy Morris, landowner J.C. Hunter Sr., John Watson and Glenn Biggs. *Courtesy Guadalupe Mountains National Park.*

When interviewed, Biggs stated that the development of the national park was "all consuming" for him, adding that he put in many extra hours and spent his own money to promote the area to those who could possibly make the difference. It is reported that Biggs would have earned a huge 5 percent commission on the sale price of $1.5 million, should he complete the sale. But he was so committed to seeing this unique land preserved that he talked landowner J.C. Hunter Jr. into considering a sale to the park service instead of a private individual.

A 1956 graduate of Baylor University, Biggs served as an assistant manager of the Abilene Chamber of Commerce, which is where he met Hunter. Once Biggs entered his career as a real estate agent, Hunter became one of his most prominent clients. Since he knew the importance of the land and his client, Biggs developed a colorful, highly attractive sales packet for the Guadalupe Mountain Ranch. Wildlife, natural resources and scenic aspects were featured in the brochure, which originally offered the property as a working sheep/goat ranch. Although the ranch was an attractive property, there were no serious buyers in the private sector.

Biggs worked tirelessly for the development of the Hunter Ranch for the park service. Many described his efforts as overzealous, but they paid off in a big way for the visitors who now enjoy the results of his obsession.

Through several important contacts—Dan Ponder, an El Paso businessman; Texas governor John Connally; and New Mexico governor Jack Campbell—Biggs garnered support for his pet project, and his dream had a starting point. After being contacted by Secretary Udall and asked whether the State of Texas had plans for the Guadalupe Mountains, Governor Connally responded that he felt the state would not be able to "undertake such a large-scale project," thus opening the door for the National Park Service.

Through the overwhelming support of the Texas and New Mexico lawmakers, and after many years of congressional visits, votes and debates, Biggs's dream of the conservation of one of the most beautiful spots in Texas came to fruition in 1972. He was present at the dedication ceremony and continued to be a huge supporter of the national park.

The Herculean efforts of all the aforementioned men have resulted in a national park that is, in the opinion of many, second to none. These men deserve a great deal of respect and a huge thank-you for their foresight, hard work and dedication.

CHAPTER 6
GUADALUPE MOUNTAINS NATIONAL PARK

As you make your drive to Guadalupe Mountains National Park, the landscape surrounding the vehicle might look a bit foreboding, arid and unwelcoming, but in truth, lush escapes lie hidden in the folds of the limestone reef.

The land itself holds great mysteries, many of which are still unsolved. Place yourself in the shoes of the early explorers as they first saw the magnificent El Capitan standing guard like a centennial over the desert kingdom below, and realize how awestruck they must have been as well.

John Russell Bartlett, friend of famed poet Edgar Allan Poe, visited the Guadalupe Mountains and was struck by the beauty he observed in the land and sunrises. Bartlett wrote about the distinctive sunrise, "No sunrise at sea or from the mountain's summit could equal in grandeur that which we now beheld, when the first rays struck the snow-clad mountain…the snow produced the most brilliant and ever-changing iris hues. No painter's art could reproduce, or colors initiate, these gorgeous prismatic tints."

Authors Paul and Susana Katz theorize that the name "Guadalupe" is a derivative of the Aztec word *Huatalope*, which means "one who treads on snakes," while others believe the mountains were named in honor of Our Lady of Guadalupe. The Spaniards named the magnificent mountains Sierra de Cenizas, which means "Ashes Mountain," most likely due to their distinctive gray color. Another story tells of a young Mexican girl, Guadalupe, who was abducted by the Apache and taken to the mountains, which were then named in her memory. Whatever the truth, the Guadalupe

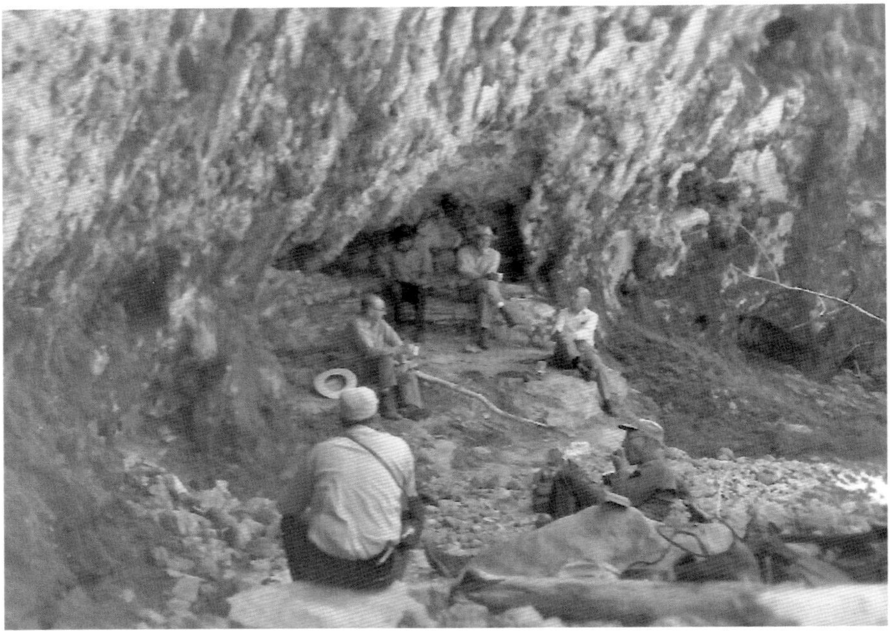

A survey party for the National Park Service Regional Office toured McKittrick Canyon to determine whether it was worthy of national park status. *From left to right*: landowner J.C. Hunter Sr., ranch foreman Noel Kincaid and National Park Service personnel T.J. Allen, G.W. Miller, L.P. Arnberger and Paul Wykert. *Courtesy Guadalupe Mountains National Park.*

Mountains have a stunning history, including their more recent struggle to become a national park.

Originally, Texas officials were considering the Guadalupe Mountains for a state park. In a report written for the Texas State Parks Board, David Obert gave several suggestions on ways to improve the region to make a pleasant experience for the park visitors, including building a "naturalistic swimming pool" in the canyon just above the present site of Hunter's Lodge.

Obert wrote that J.C. Hunter wanted to give Texas only two sections of land, which would encompass McKittrick Canyon and some of the high land above the area. He stated, "I do not want to belittle the Judge's generosity, but I feel that the two sections in that country, for park purposes, is 'like the proverbial wart on the back of a hog.'" Obert's suggestion leaned toward a more substantial land donation that would be large enough to make a township.

Later in Obert's report, he suggested that McKittrick Canyon be made to attract people to stay no less than two weeks—to be made into somewhere that people could dine and dance, swim, play tennis, ride horses, hike and fish while having accommodations such as cabins and rooms available for lodging purposes.

By the end of his report, however, it appeared that Obert changed his mind. While he noted that McKittrick Canyon had the potential to be the finest state park in Texas, he ultimately suggested leaving the canyon as it was:

> *It would be far better to leave this beautiful canyon as it is, than to mar it with over-development, and unless the state can acquire enough land to control development in the canyon, a road built into it is going to encourage private enterprise and exploration that will forever destroy much of its freshness and beauty for the people of Texas and the Nation.*

The automobile played a large part in the development of the nation's national park system. It was popular to drive in motorcades across the country to see the sights. In the 1920s, no direct highway existed between Carlsbad, New Mexico, and El Paso, Texas. Travelers had to go through the Sacramento Mountains by means of Artesia, Hope, Cloudcroft and Alamogordo, New Mexico, to access El Paso. In 1927, a wealthy business owner from El Paso decided there needed to be a more direct route and put $5,000 toward the project while challenging others to do the same.

Wallace Pratt owned over 16,000 acres of land in the Guadalupe Mountains by 1937 and generously donated 5,632 acres to the National Park Service for the preservation of the land that included McKittrick land.

It took over fifty years for the Guadalupe Mountains National Park to see fruition. Government and private efforts were often met with disdain and controversy, but eventually, on October 15, 1966, the park was born when Congress passed "An Act to Provide for the Establishment of the Guadalupe Mountains National Park in the State of Texas." The act stated, in part:

> *Be it enacted by the Senate and House of Representatives of the United States of America in Congress assembled, that, in order to preserve in public ownership an area in the State of Texas possessing outstanding geological values together with scenic and other natural values of great significance, the Secretary of the Interior shall establish the Guadalupe Mountains National Park.*

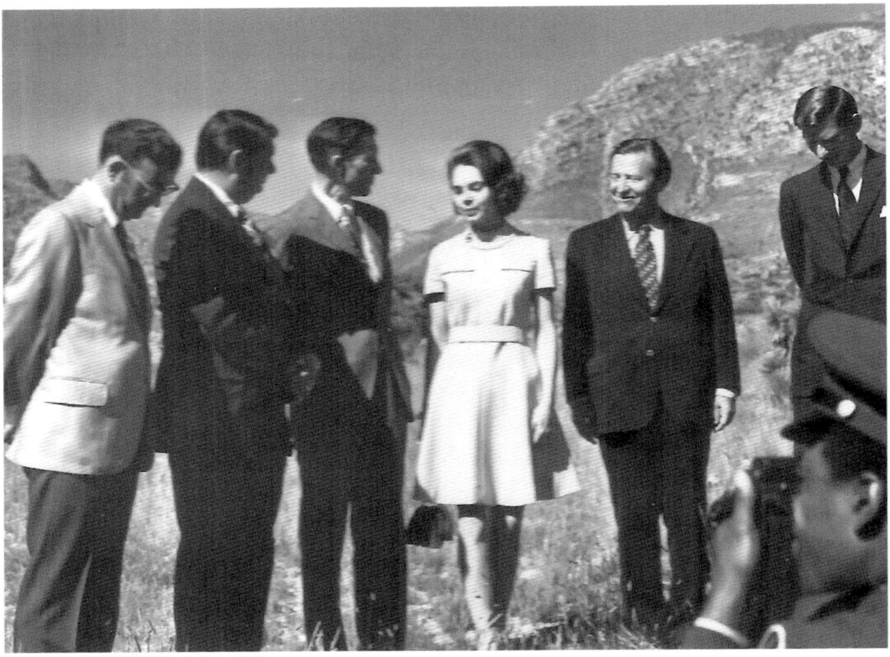

On September 30, 1972, many dignitaries gathered at the Frijole Ranch to dedicate the Guadalupe Mountains. *From left to right*: Superintendent Dayton, Stanley Hulett, Representative R.A. White, Julie Nixon Eisenhower, Ralph W. Yarborough and Nathaniel Reed. *Courtesy Guadalupe Mountains National Park.*

The official opening of the park would not occur until September 30, 1972, when dignitaries such as first daughter Julie Nixon Eisenhower, who would deliver the keynote speech, and Nathaniel Reed, assistant secretary for Fish and Wildlife and Parks, were on site to dedicate the new park into the National Park System in front of 2,400 attendees.

The park is part of the Trans-Pecos Region, a physiographic region that is home to many mountain ranges, including the Guadalupe, Delaware, Davis, Apache, Glass, Santiago, Chalk, Christmas, Chisos, Van Horn, Hueco, Franklin, Sierra Vieja, Chinati, Finlay and Quitman Mountains, as well as the Toyah and Marathon Basins and the Diablo Plateau.

The most distinctive feature of the Guadalupe Mountains is a limestone formation that goes by several names. Called Cathedral Rock by the Spanish explorers who traveled through the Chihuahuan Desert because of the visible cross carved into its face by the chisel of nature, El Capitan was used as a navigational landmark by early travelers, as well as an "all-weather post" by airplane pilots. El Capitan is visible for fifty miles from many directions, and Guadalupe Peak, located directly behind it, is also known as Signal Peak since it was thought to be used by the natives to communicate with one another. The Apache also called the imposing rock formation Rock Nose, most likely because of its distinctive shape.

Dallas Morning News columnist Frank X. Tolbert, an enthusiastic supporter of the Guadalupe Mountains, and particularly McKittrick Canyon, once wrote that El Capitan was "one of the biggest exposed fossil reefs in the world," adding that "the morning and late afternoon sun makes gorgeous dyes on its yellow face."

New York Herald reporter W.L. Ormsby, who traveled the Butterfield Overland Mail Route from New York to San Francisco in 1858, described El Capitan thusly: "It seems as if Nature had saved up all her ruggedness to pile it up in this colossal form."

The mountains first came into play when the overland mail contract was awarded to wealthy investor John Butterfield in 1857. Since childhood, Butterfield, who was born in Utica, New York, had always wanted to be a stagecoach driver. He accomplished this goal with such bravado that he was soon made manager of the line and started his own lines, which would eventually be converted to railroads.

With the $600,000 contract secure, Butterfield set out to complete a feat many thought impossible—ferry mail nearly three thousand miles from San Francisco, California, to St. Louis, Missouri, in twenty-five days with only two stagecoaches per week. Butterfield built the longest coach line in the world in only one year. His coaches were called "mudders" or "mud wagons" due to the fact that they were basically open-air cabs with only canvas flaps, which could be rolled up or down, to protect the passengers from the elements. Excellent vehicles for the rough roads the drivers encountered in the Guadalupe Mountains, they held anywhere from six to twelve people and were made by the Abbott-Downing Company of Concord, New Hampshire.

On September 28, 1858, the westbound stage from St. Louis and the eastbound stage originating in San Francisco passed each other on the trail at the 5,534-foot elevation of Guadalupe Pass in the Guadalupe Mountains. Passengers and drivers took a few moments to exchange pleasantries and went on their way into history. This pass is still being utilized by modern traffic today.

Passage for the entire trip was $200, or $0.15 per mile. Unfortunately, the trip was rough through the arid parts of the country, causing reporter

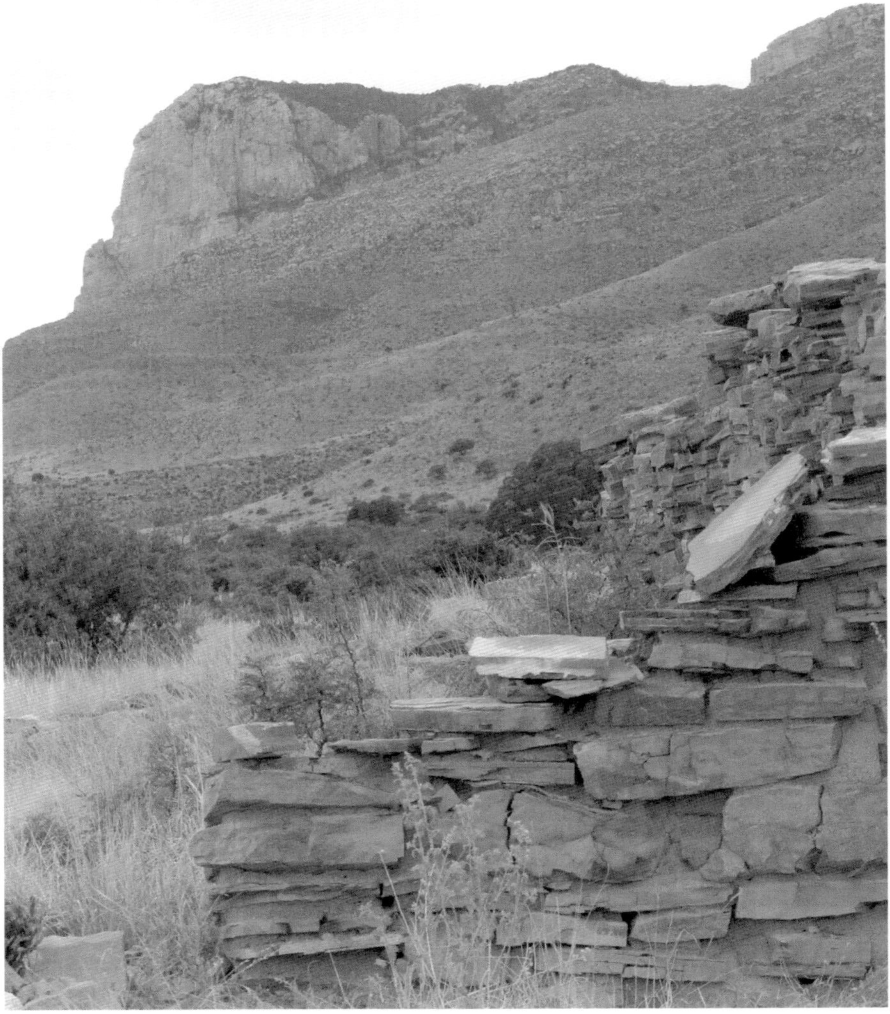

Above and opposite: Stand close to the remnants of the Butterfield stage station, and you can almost hear the whispers of the past. *Author's collection*.

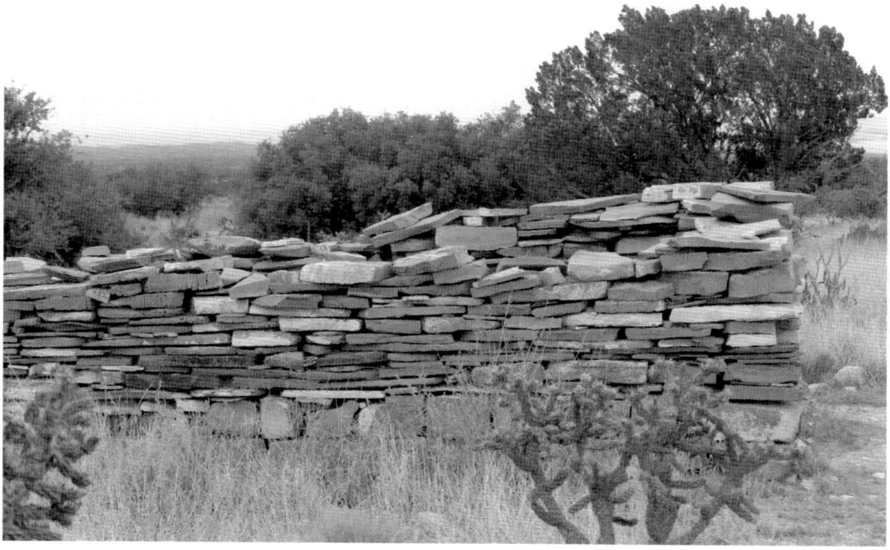

W.L. Ormsby III, the first passenger to complete the entire trip, to describe it as "a trip through hell." Traveling an average of 120 miles per day at 5 miles per hour allowed the 2,800-mile cross-country trek to be completed in approximately twenty-five to twenty-eight days, depending on weather and trail conditions.

One of the stops along the way was the Pinery Station, which at first existed as only a rock corral. The Pinery crew lived in tents and, for the most part, lived off the land, hunting deer and other livestock. Pine Springs was called the "Point of the Mountain" by locals and government officials alike. Water was the most important of elements at the station. Using an *acequia*, or open ditch, the crew funneled water from Pine Springs to a tank located in the northwest corner of the Pinery. The stone corral at the station boasted walls that were approximately five feet tall, while a rock wall surrounding the entire station was built eleven feet tall and thirty inches thick to act as a fortress against the marauding tribes in the area. Although successful, the Pinery Station would close in 1861, just nine months after opening, due to the line being cut during the Civil War.

In 1907, this land was purchased by an individual named Walter Glover, who, along with his wife, Bertha, ran a small country store/café at the foot of El Capitan. Glover knew the Guadalupe Mountains like the back of his hand and would relay many stories of the area, as well as his escapades as a Texas Ranger, to his customers. Pine Springs Café was the oldest operation

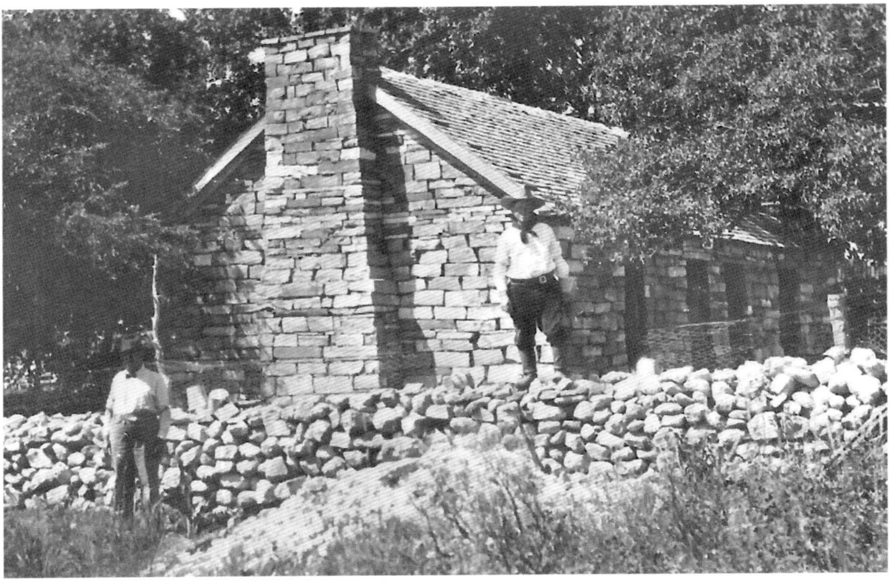

Walter Glover bought the land at what would become Pine Springs, Texas, in 1907 to start a ranch. When Highway 62/180 was built, it became the highest roadway in Texas, at an elevation of 5,695 feet. By 1928, Glover and his wife, Bertha, had opened a store/café at this spot. The café would remain open until Bertha's death in 1982. The Glover family would be one of the last holdbacks to the progression of Guadalupe Mountains National Park. *Courtesy Guadalupe Mountains National Park.*

of its kind on the highway that was still owned by an original family member, the Glovers having been in the area for over seventy-five years.

During the land struggle with the United States government in the 1960s, Glover became distrustful of government officials, who were, in his opinion, trying to steal his land to create the national park. Anyone who wore a suit was immediately viewed as a government official and was treated with disdain. After 85.8 acres of Glover's land, including the Butterfield Stage Station and some family-owned land dating back to 1913, was acquired in 1972 through condemnation proceedings and subsequent court settlements, the United States government gave back a few of the rights to the land. The Glover family had the right to remain and operate the store/café for the rest of their lives, and when Walter passed away in 1973, that right passed down to his wife, Bertha. Bertha passed in 1982, and the right was then handed down to their daughter, Mary Henson, who asked to stay on the property for a short time. The main café property, which once had the skin of a six-foot rattlesnake hanging over the front door, was demolished in October 1982.

Mary Henson had moved into a concrete structure on the property, which she would vacate in 1984. When asked to describe the two-story, twenty-one- by thirty-two-foot former dance hall, Henson said, "It ain't pretty, but it's hell for stout."

The bill by Congressman Richard C. White, a Democrat from El Paso, Texas, created the park in 1966. Today, the Guadalupe Mountains National Park encompasses 135 square miles, with 80 of those miles being hiking trails. There are also nine permanent springs on the parkland. None of this would have been possible if Texas governor John Connally had not relinquished the water and mineral rights included in the acreage to the U.S. government in 1967.

Joe Markley, the manager of the Midland Division of the Texaco Corporation, relinquished all mineral rights to the park in 1967, overcoming the last obstacle before development of the park could begin. Congressman White noted:

> *This is the most significant development since the Texas legislature approved the transfer of the mineral rights of the State of Texas in the Guadalupe Mountains area. West Texas now may anticipate the establishment of this important National Park within a short time. Texaco has again proven itself a good citizen of West Texas, recognizing the great benefits, recreation, tourist trade and national recognition that will come through our area as a result of this National Park. It was the last barrier, and I hope the federal government is ready now to begin development of this park site that I think is one of the most beautiful anywhere.*

The Texaco Corporation also decided to donate ten thousand acres of its own landholdings in the Guadalupe Mountains to the park. President Lyndon B. Johnson was then asked for $1.8 million for the development of the Guadalupe Mountains National Park.

Also in 1967, the Texas School Land Board members signed the Guadalupe Park land deed granting 47,895 acres of land to the park. A permanent school fund was to be paid five dollars per acre for the mineral rights out of a special appropriation made to Texas state treasurer Jesse James by the legislature.

The original deed, which resides in the State of Texas Archives, with duplicate copies in Hudspeth and Culberson Counties, is a beautiful document bound in red leather and lettered with red, blue and black ink. Designed by Miss Eltea Armstrong, an artist for the General Land Office, the cover was decorated with a drawing of El Capitan. Part of the original deed states if the United States fails to maintain the park, the mineral rights will revert back to the State of Texas immediately. Additionally, the state is to share in the proceeds should the land ever be used for the development of oil and gas, which would occur only in an extreme national emergency.

During the construction of the Guadalupe Mountains National Park, problems arose that would delay the project by two years. Southwest Region hydraulic engineer Garland Moore found water in the park in 1974 while park planners were searching for a supply source for all of the anticipated expansion. Having planned to drill to 5,000 feet, Moore was thrilled to find a good water source at 2,673 feet and completed the well that year.

Guadalupe Mountains National Park remains the only legally designated wilderness area in West Texas and contains four of the highest geographical points in Texas. The park encompasses Culberson and Hudspeth Counties in Texas, as well as Eddy, Otero and Chaves Counties in New Mexico. Guadalupe Peak rises an impressive 8,751 feet above the desert floor and has understandably been given the nickname the "Top o' Texas."

The National Park Service reminds all who visit its beautiful parks that the removal of any material from the park is strictly prohibited. A visitor who takes an artifact, fossil or other item might downplay its significance, but remember, this is one more thing that future visitors will not get to experience.

CHAPTER 7

HIKING TRAILS

Whether you are a beginner or a seasoned hiker, McKittrick Canyon provides a wealth of trails that have been written about in many distinguished hiking journals the world over. The trails in the main part of the canyon itself tend to be rocky (they generally follow riverbeds and have been described by some hikers as like walking on a bed of golf balls), so one tip is to always wear good boots that provide foot and ankle support. It is also suggested that you bring sunscreen, a hat, a map and weather gear, since the weather is known to change on a dime from many extremes in the mountains.

In addition to developing and maintaining the trails, in some areas, the National Park Service has even provided a series of stairs carved out of the native rock to advance the hiker through the canyon.

Designated as a day use–only park, McKittrick Canyon is in the Mountain Daylight Time (MDT) zone and is open from 8:00 a.m. to 6:00 p.m. April–October and from 8:00 a.m. to 4:30 p.m. November–March. The park service locks the entrance gate every evening. As with any national park, there is an entrance fee, which is to be paid before entering the canyon. As part of the honor system, simply place your envelope with the allotted fee in a box at the trailhead. Like any government agency, budget cuts can affect the amount of personnel, equipment and supplies that a national park receives. Paying the fee helps ensure that our national parks remain accessible to the public so that everyone can enjoy them for many years to come.

With any outdoor adventure, the absolute first rule is to stay hydrated. At McKittrick Canyon, you must carry in your own water, as none will be available

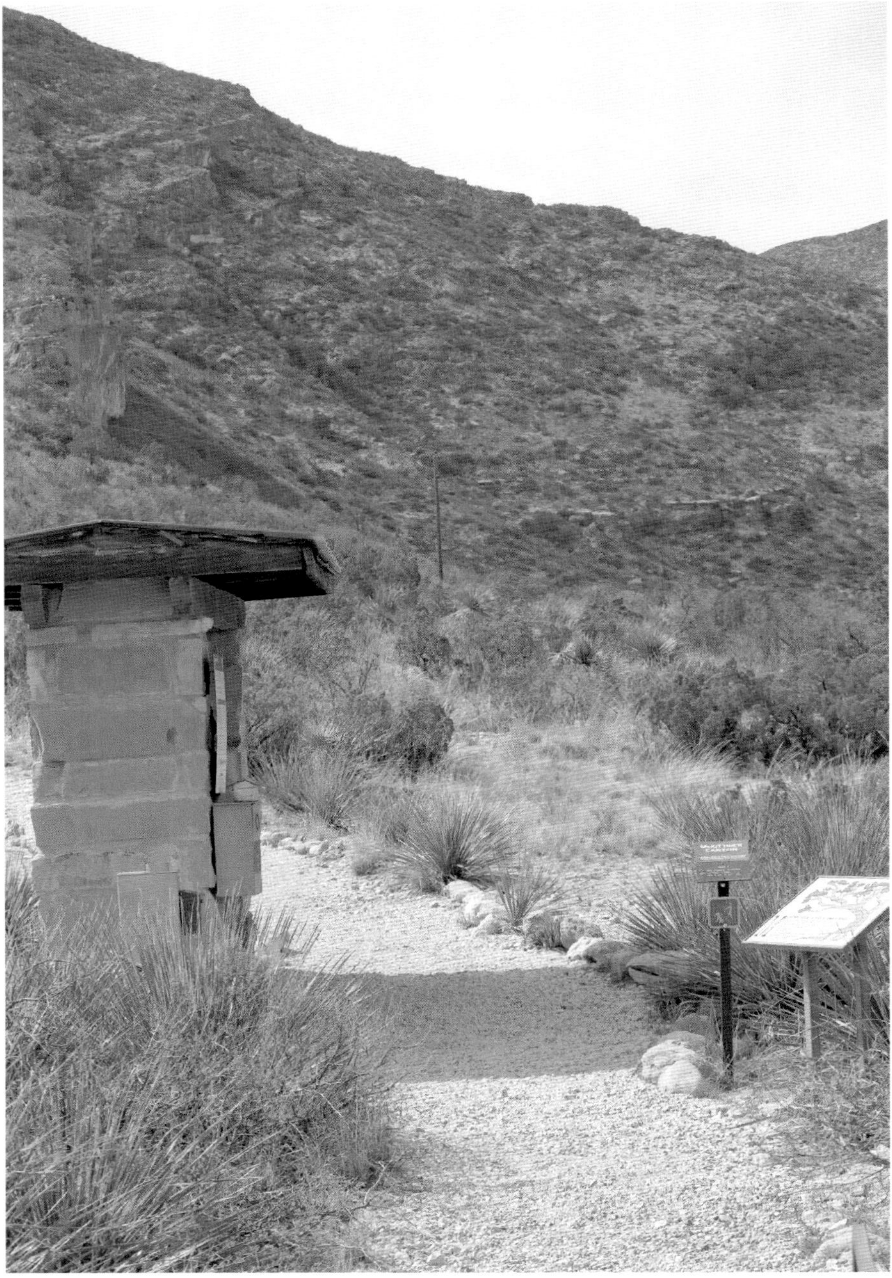

When starting your journey, be sure to sign in at the McKittrick Canyon Trailhead logbook and pay your nominal five-dollar fee. This gives you seven days of hiking privileges, should you choose to return for another hike. *Author's collection.*

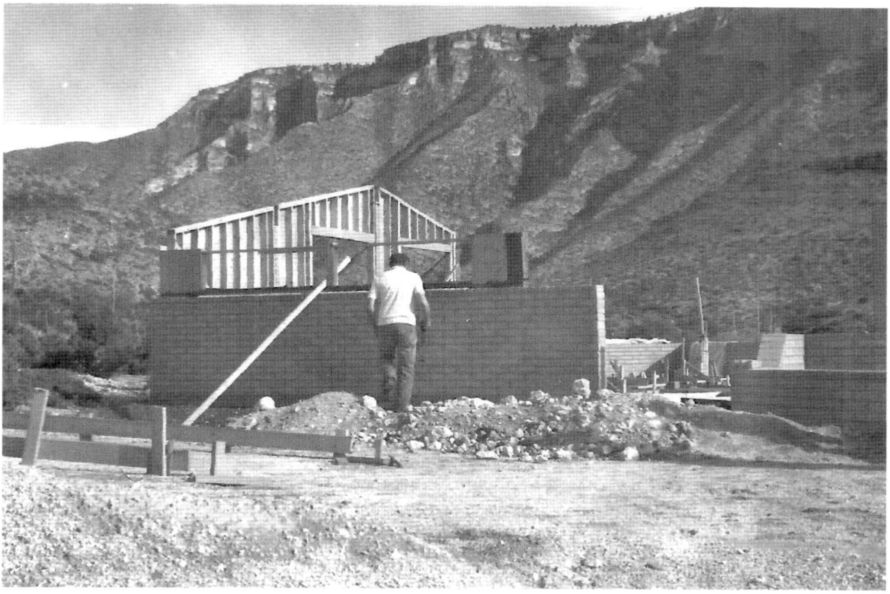

The McKittrick Canyon Visitors' Center was a small travel trailer that served as the rangers' station until construction on the new building was complete. *Courtesy Guadalupe Mountains National Park.*

after you leave the visitors' center. The recommended amount is one gallon per person, which can be a bit heavy to carry at first; however, you will be overjoyed you made the extra effort as your body adjusts to the 5,013-foot elevation and the dry climate of the high desert and wants relief.

McKittrick Canyon Nature Trail

The McKittrick Canyon Nature Trail is a short, often-forgotten trail that begins to the left of the parking area, trailhead and visitors' center. The .9-mile trail, which is rated moderate and takes a little under an hour to complete, provides a brief overview of what hikers will experience in the longer jaunts. Wildlife often gathers in this quiet area to escape the number of visitors McKittrick Canyon sometimes attracts. This trail is a great educational tool that can be used to illustrate the different types of plants and animals that reside in the canyon. It features many plants found in the scrub desert, including faxon yucca, ocotillo, sotol and many species of cacti.

The National Park Service brochure notes, "It seems impossible for anything to grow in such harsh conditions, yet the plants have evolved to meet the challenge." Ranger Elizabeth Fields tells visitors, "The nature trail is a great way to see some of the many birds and plants represented in the canyon without having to take a strenuous hike. You don't even need hiking boots."

South McKittrick Canyon Hiking Trail

The South McKittrick Canyon Hiking Trail is the shortest and most popular hiking trail at the park. The 4.8-mile trail starts at the visitors' center, follows the McKittrick Canyon Creek bed in the heart of the canyon and ends at Stone Cabin (Pratt Cabin). This is the most traveled path, especially during the fall months, when the vegetation is putting on a spectacular show. Do not be surprised if you see a family of mule deer strolling along just beyond the perimeter of the trail beside you. It might be tempting to feed the deer, but please refrain from doing so, as it will upset the delicate balance in the canyon.

Former Carlsbad Municipal School librarian and Guadalupe Mountains National Park volunteer Carol Belski shared an experience she had while hiking the canyon during the colors tour, which is usually held in late October or early November. Having hiked this trail for many years, one can become almost immune to the beauty that surrounds you, but on this one particular day, everything changed. "There was a particularly thick fog enveloping the canyon, and all that was visible were the rain-soaked leaves," recalled Carol. "The red, orange and yellow leaves were dripping with beads of moisture. The canopy of fog erased the rest of the canyon, and it gave me a new, surreal experience."

At Stone Cabin, there are picnic areas where you can stop, enjoy a gentle breeze and eat a bite before traveling on or returning to the visitors' center. Remember, the canyon is part of the Guadalupe Mountains National Park, and in order to maintain the canyon in its present pristine manner, whatever you carry into the park—food wrappers, water bottles, etc.—must also be carried back out. This rule is strictly enforced to ensure the future enjoyment of others who will also be visiting the canyon, as well as to protect the fragile environment within the canyon.

Unfortunately, due to devastating floods in September 2013 and 2014, the picnic area that was located along the left side of the ascending trail has

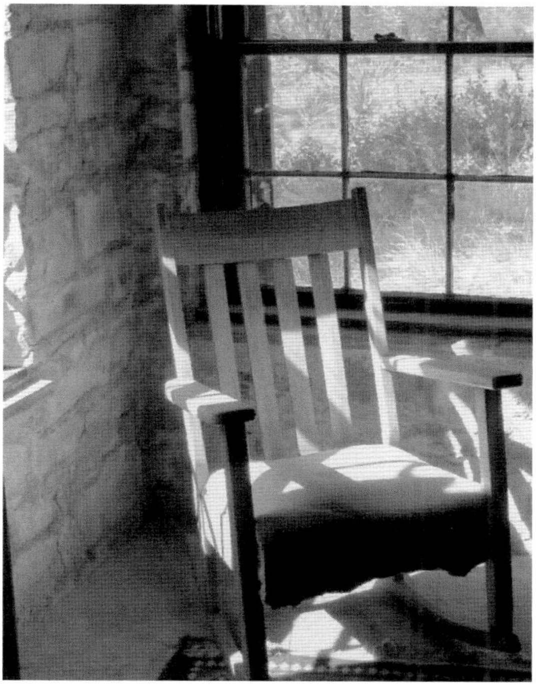

Right: One can imagine Wallace Pratt sitting in this rocking chair and reading a good book while soaking up the outstanding views that surrounded his home. *Author's collection.*

Below: Hunter's Lodge provided a peaceful respite for guests who came to McKittrick Canyon for hunting trips hosted by J.C. Hunter Sr. *Author's collection.*

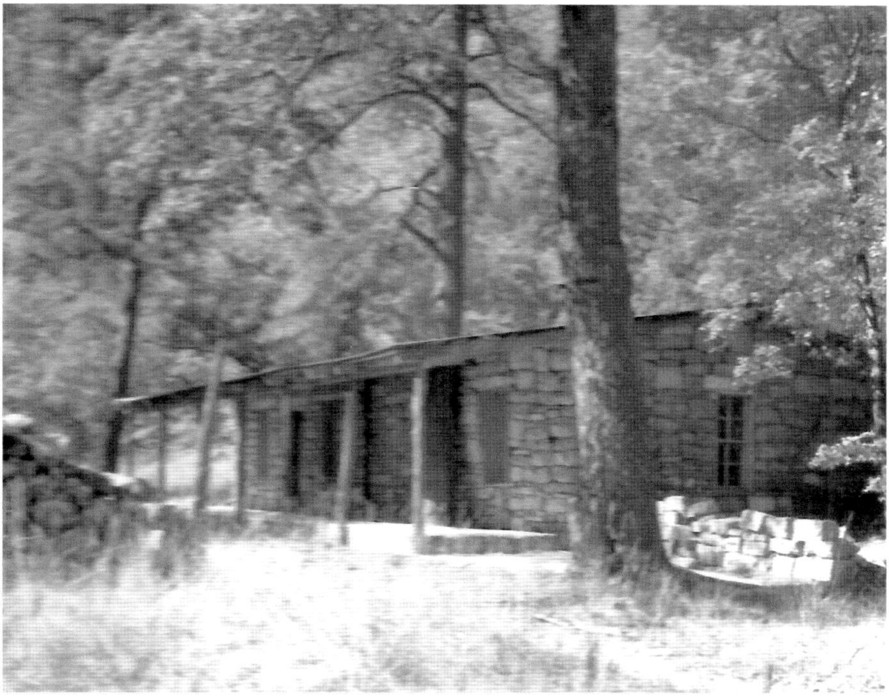

been obliterated. But if you make the turn to the right and walk the short distance to the cabin, you can still relax under a massive Texas madrone that was probably there when the Pratt family first built their cabin.

After your respite, continue up the trail to the grotto, a shallow cave surrounded by large slate picnic tables where hikers can rest or grab a fast bite before finishing their trek. This leg of the trail provides some of the most spectacular foliage and is well worth the extra hike. The grotto area also shows evidence that the canyon might have been covered like the Carlsbad Caverns at one time, as huge boulders scattered along the creek bed provide hikers with something to lean against if they need to rest or rebuild their strength. Created by dripping water filtering through limestone, which forms calcium carbonate, the grotto forms a miniature cave complete with stalagmites and stalactites, much like its much larger sister to the north.

Approximately seven hundred feet up the trail from the grotto is what is commonly known as Hunter's Lodge. A flagstone structure much like Pratt's Stone Cabin, it is the end of the line for this spur of the trail. In the past, J.C. Hunter used this lodge as a line shack or as a place for people to stay while visiting on hunting trips or sightseeing tours. Unoccupied except for a family of bats, the lodge is a picturesque reminder of an easier time.

North McKittrick Canyon Hiking Trail

Before reaching the grotto, a fork in the trail will give you a choice of visiting the grotto or going to the right for a more strenuous hike into North McKittrick Canyon. This trail will take you through more fabulous displays of fall colors during that season. If you decide to continue for the rest of the trail, you will hike along the top of the ridge and pass through "the Notch," where you will cross over into New Mexico and Dog Canyon on the opposite side of the mountain. This is a strenuous, 14.8-mile hike and will take many hours of continuous walking to complete. It is also the steepest trail in the park and the only place in the McKittrick Canyon system where you are allowed to camp overnight. A camping permit may be obtained from the visitors' center, located just to the right of the highway near El Capitan at Pine Springs.

Permian Reef Geology Trail

For more adventurous hikers, the Permian Reef Geology Trail, described by the National Park Service as a trail for "serious geology buffs," provides a definite challenge. Rising to elevations of over two thousand feet above the canyon floor, the 8.4-mile switchback trail offers a steep ascent to the bottom of the escarpment. Numbered stops along the trail correspond with a brochure that is available at the visitors' center.

The trail is considered to be strenuous because of the sharp, gravelly ascent, but with good hiking boots, a walking stick and plenty of water, a hiker will be prepared to take on the challenge. The views from the top of the ridge as you look down into McKittrick Canyon are well worth the efforts.

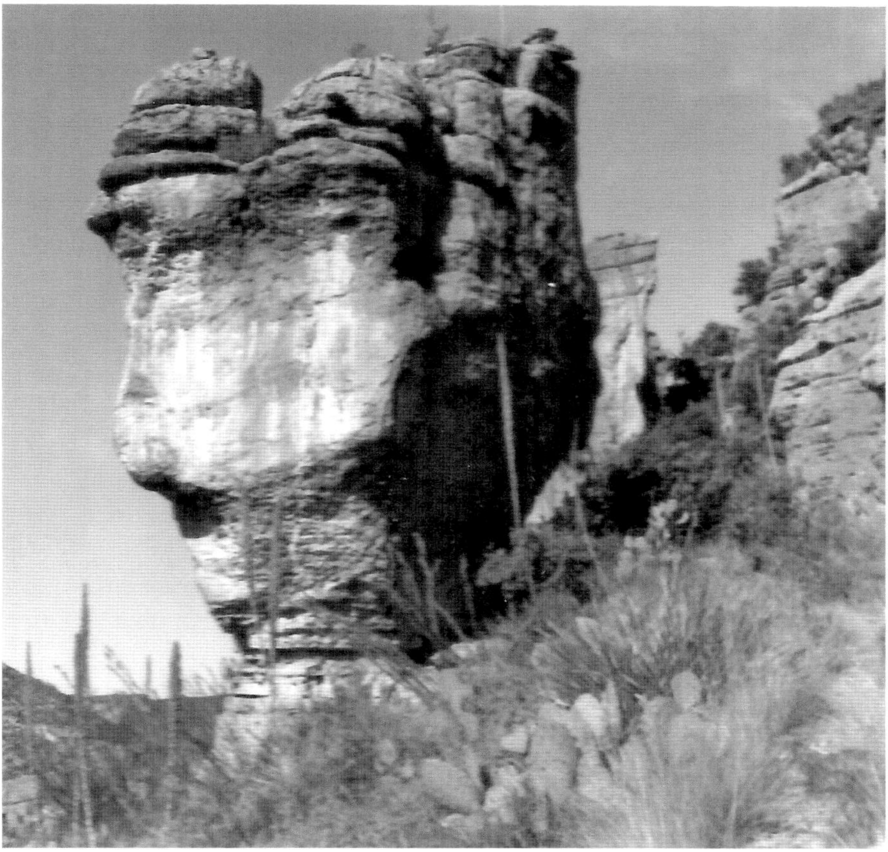

Although a strenuous trek, the Permian Basin Geology Trail has many exciting rock formations to witness. *Courtesy Guadalupe Mountains National Park.*

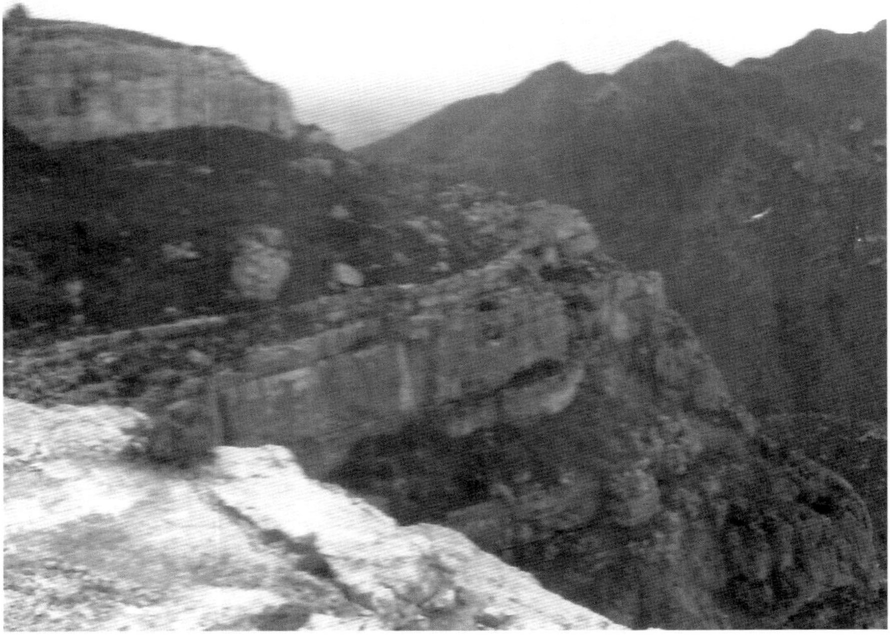

Breathtaking views into McKittrick Canyon await you from the top of the Permian Basin Trail. *Courtesy Guadalupe Mountains National Park.*

Due to the difficulty, it is suggested that hikers take the trip in short intervals, starting early in the morning, and rest often. Bring a sack lunch to be enjoyed about halfway to the top at the overhang—the views of McKittrick Canyon and the Permian Basin are spectacular and well worth the possibility of blisters to witness. As with all the Guadalupe Mountains National Park system, take nothing and leave only your footprints.

As you begin your journey across the dry bed of McKittrick Creek, you will encounter beds of sedimentary rock that appear to be cemented together. Called conglomerates, these formations were created during the last ice age, approximately forty thousand years ago, when floods carried the stones to their current location, tumbling them smooth and round in the process.

The next area will reveal outcrops of chert nodules, otherwise called flint. These nodules are made of silica and are more resistant to erosion than their limestone hosts. The Native Americans used these stones to make arrowheads, beads and hand tools. Chert flakes are some of the most common objects in an archaeological site.

According to the Permian Reef trail guide produced by the National Park Service, "Every rock provides a clue to the forces that have shaped the land." A good example of this is boundstone, which was formed by algae that grew around sponges in the Permian Sea. The fact that examples of this stone are found at the beginning of the trail is a good indication as to the force of waves and currents that churned the ancient seas. Fossils such as worm borrows, brachiopods, fusulinids, ammonoids, bryozoans, sponges, collenellas and stromatolites also make up a major portion of the reef. Formed mostly by algae, these creatures are the cement that holds the Capitan Reef structure together.

Along the trail, you will encounter large stone formations that resemble the heads on Easter Island. Created by the erosion of millions of years of flooding and general weather conditions, the burrowed wackestone formations stand proud.

At the highest point of the trail, you will be standing two thousand feet above sea level and have an amazing view of not only McKittrick Canyon but also the Permian Basin below.

CHAPTER 8

FLORA AND FAUNA OF THE CANYON

As you walk along the peaceful paths in McKittrick Canyon, it is easy to miss the subtle beauty that is always at your feet. Be sure to look down at the tiny sprigs of wildflowers and cacti tucked amid the wisps of sawgrass (*Cladium jamaicense*) that line the trails, as well as the delicate and rare pink rose (*Rosa woodsii*) that grows along the side of the trail and usually blooms in May.

According to the National Park Service, the plants of McKittrick Canyon are broken down into three biotic communities: desert, evergreen woodlands and primal forests. This diversity seems to defy all traditional modes of floristic classifications. This unique canyon is home to varieties of plants that are normally found in other parts of the country or world, such as the chinquapin oak (*Quercus muhlenbergii*), whose origin is in the New England states, as well as the Bulbert fern, which is a native of Newfoundland. The canyon is also home to an isolated species of moss, *Venturiella sinensis var. angustiannulata*, which occurs in only two other spots, China and a small refugium in Oklahoma.

There are actually six varieties of animals and twelve varieties of plants that are thought to be rare in the region. Scientists believe the main reason for these occurrences are due to the fact that the region was cooler and less arid thousands of years ago, and adaptation transpired.

Plants that thrive in the desert community are the creosote cush (*Larrea tridentate*), which gives off a wonderful fresh smell after a rainstorm; algerita or barberry (*Berberis sp.*); Mexican orange (*Choisya dumosa*); desert buckhorn

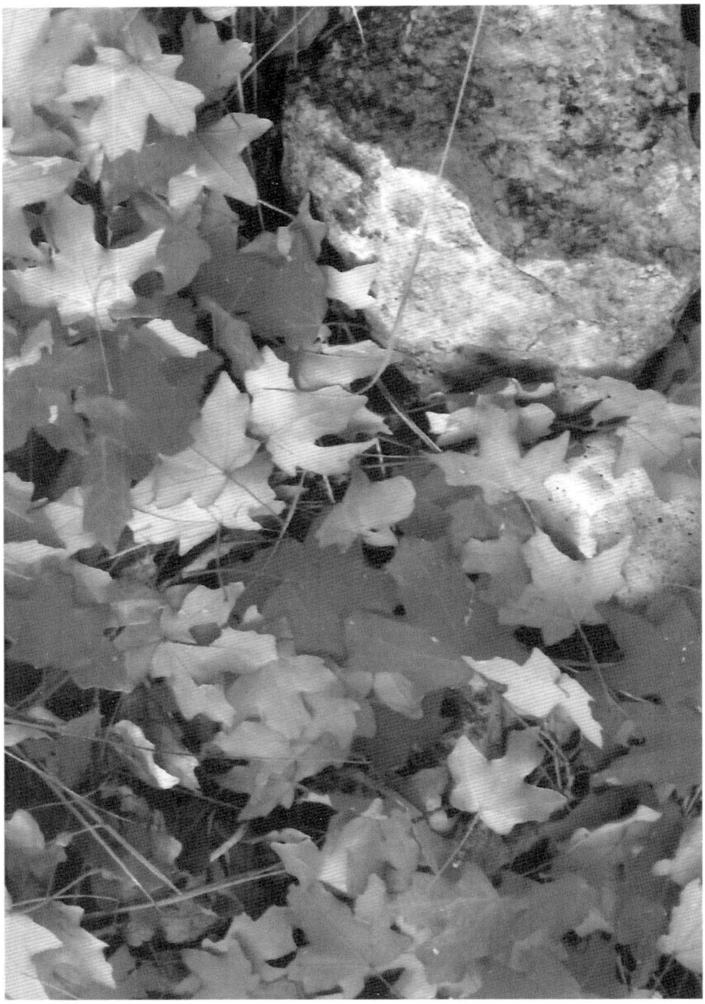

As you walk along the meandering canyon trail, you will notice the carpet of leaves, oak and maple being the most prominent. *Author's collection.*

(*Ceanothus greggii*); tarbush (*Fourensia cernua*); mountain mahogany (*Cercocarpus montanus*); western honey mesquite (*Prosopsis glandulosa*); acacia (*Acacia neovernicosa*); desert sumac (*Rhus triobata*); Apache plume (*Fallugia paradoxa*); four-winged salt bush, also known as chamiza (*Atriplex canescens*); and grama grass (*Bouteloua eriopoda*).

Other unexpected plants that grow in the more arid regions of the canyon include the prickly pear (*Opuntia engelmannii*); ocotillo (*Fouquiera splendens*)

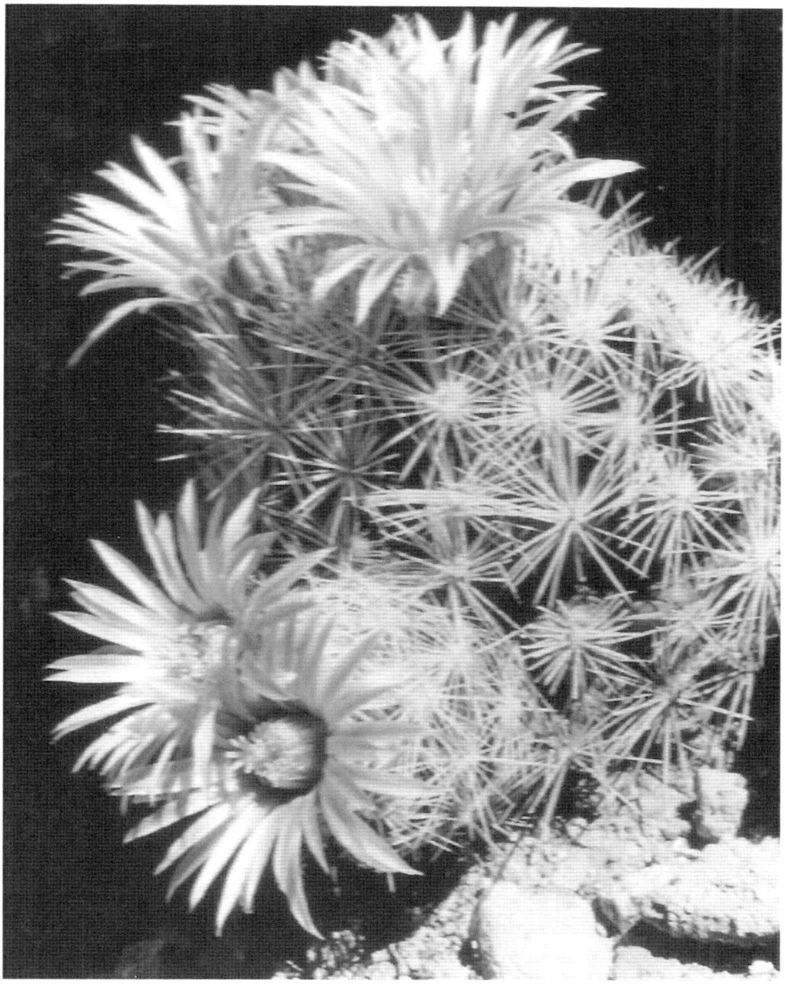

This stunning example of a *Coryphantha vivipara*, commonly known as a spiny star, was photographed on the top of the escarpment of McKittrick Canyon in 1963. *Courtesy Guadalupe Mountains National Park.*

(pronounced oh-ko-TEE-oh); lechuguilla (*Agave lechuguilla*) (pronounced letch-you-GHEE-ah); claret cup cactus, which is sometimes called strawberry hedgehog (*Echinocereus triglochidiatus*); and cholla (*Opuntia imbricate*) (pronounced CHOY-ya), which dots the landscape and sometimes clings to rock ledges on the canyon walls.

The cholla has a self-pruning mechanism wherein the arms of the plant are segmented and drop off voluntarily, earning it the nickname "jumping cholla." Their spines are treacherous and will stick to anything passing by, be it animal or human.

Another variety of cacti that is both dangerous and beautiful is known as horse crippler or devil's head (*Echinocactus texensis*). Generally found growing in tall grasses, this variety is low to the ground and virtually invisible until stepped on. This desert succulent prevents drying out by storing water in the delicate tissues under its dangerous thorns.

The Guadalupe Mountains violet (*Viola guadalupenis*), a small, yellow-flowered perennial violet, is an extremely rare endemic plant found only in the high-elevation limestone faces in the Guadalupe Mountains.

Many tree varieties are scattered along the canyon bed, including black walnut (*Juglans nigra*), Mexican buckeye (*Ungnadia speciosa*), velvet ash (*Fraxinus velutina*), Texas madrone (*Arbutus texana*), bigtooth maple (*Acer grandidentatum*), gray oak (*Quercus grisea*), alligator juniper (*Juniperus sp.*) and piñon (*Pinus edulis*).

With 40 species of nesting birds in McKittrick Canyon alone and over 289 species of birds in the Guadalupe Mountains National Park, the region is known as a birder's paradise. The more common species, such as the Scott's oriole, Harris's hawk or black-throated sparrow, can readily be seen along your journey through the canyon, but look closer and you will find many other varieties, including turkey vultures, golden eagles, roadrunners, owls, red-tailed hawks, ladder-backed woodpeckers, white-winged doves, wrens, scaled blue quails, northern mockingbirds, blue-grey gnatcatchers, grey vireos and several species of hummingbirds. The riparian areas provide food and protection for the birds and wildlife and serve as a breeding habitat for the Mexican spotted owl (*Strix occidentalis lucida*). The canyon walls also provide an excellent nesting site for the peregrine falcon (*Falco peregrinus*).

Although rare, mountain lions (*Puma concolor*) have been sighted in the canyon. It is generally in times of extreme drought that the cats will wander into the park area in search of the water and deer that are present. There are fifty-eight species of mammals living within the park boundaries, many of which live in McKittrick Canyon and are nocturnal. The many caves in the Guadalupe Mountains provide habitats for the sixteen varieties of bats that inhabit the canyon, including the most common species, the Mexican free-tailed bat (*Tadarida brasilensis*), which is also known as the Brazilian free-tailed bat, and the big brown bat (*Eptesicus fuscus*). Other nocturnal inhabitants that are rarely seen by visitors but leave evidence of their presence are coyotes (*Canis latrans*), bobcats (*Felis rufus*) and raccoons (*Procyon lotor*).

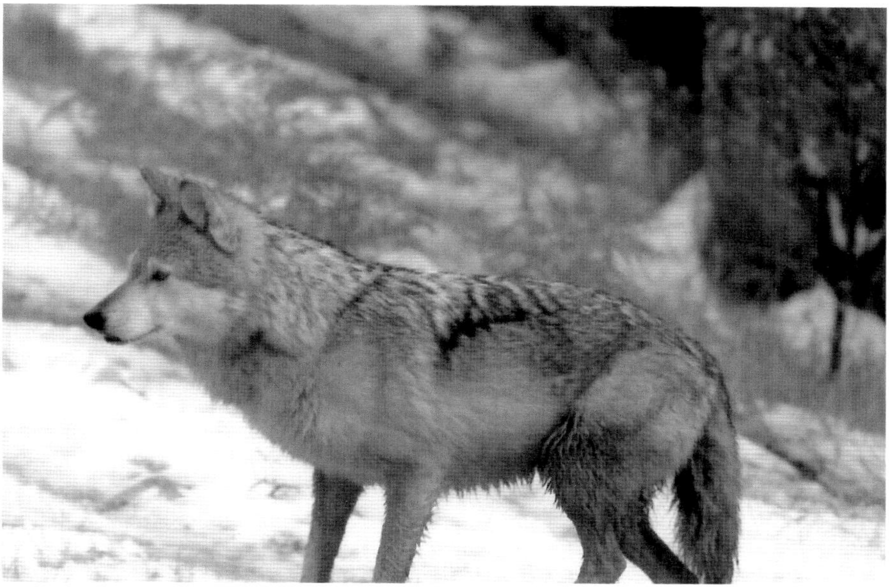

Although endangered today, the Mexican gray wolf was prevalent in the Guadalupe Mountains when the first explorers made their presence known. *Author's collection.*

Wildlife reports state that Mexican brown bears, otherwise known as pig-nosed bears, and even grizzly bears were plentiful in the Guadalupes up until the early 1920s. Other species that once roamed the canyon but are now long gone include bison, Mexican gray wolves, black-tailed prairie dogs and white-tailed deer.

J.C. Hunter introduced a small herd of forty-two Merriam's elk, which are now extinct, into the canyon in 1929. This number eventually grew so large that Hunter had to bring in his friends and colleagues to help thin out the population. Ancestors of these herds, mixed with the native Rocky Mountain elk, are still wandering the Guadalupe Mountains today. In the 1930s, Hunter was also responsible for the introduction of a flock of wild turkey as well as mountain sheep into McKittrick Canyon.

Mule deer are quite prevalent in the mountain range, as well as in nearby Carlsbad, New Mexico. Over the years, the deer have become quite accustomed to people and appear to be almost tame, remaining close to the trails as hikers pass by. The National Park Service is adamant that hikers refrain from interacting with and especially feeding the wildlife. Human food is not intended for wildlife consumption.

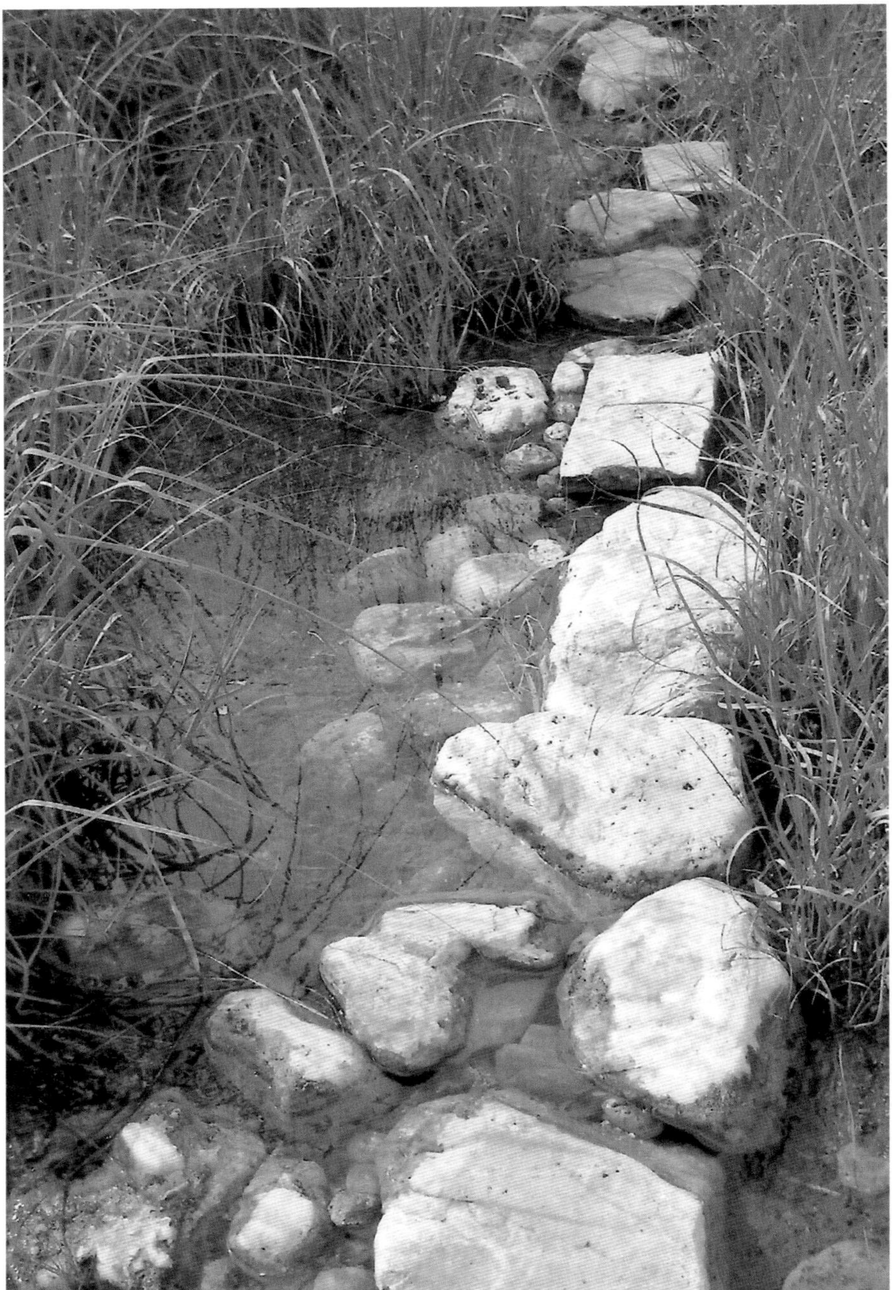

Above and opposite: McKittrick Creek is the lifeblood of the canyon, providing water and food for the plants, animals and humans that call the canyon home. *Author's collection.*

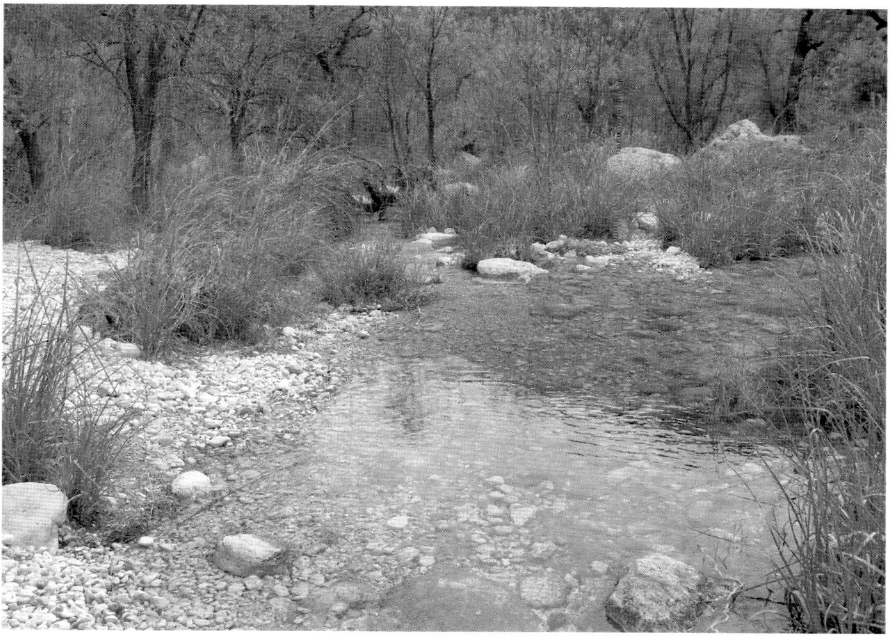

Upon close inspection of the free-flowing stream, you will notice rainbow trout, introduced to the area in 1947 by J.C. Hunter, and long-eared sunfish.

One of the only drawbacks to Hunter introducing new species into the area was the presence of Angora goats, which overgrazed the north and west sectors of the ranch. Drift fences had to be used to create a separation between the animals and the more scenic areas.

One of the biggest surprises for visitors to McKittrick Canyon is the amount of spectacular plant life that populates the canyon. The fall season is the most popular time to visit, as the leaves of the oak, bigtooth maple (*Acer grandidentatum*), rare Texas madrone (*Arbutus xalapensis*) and littleleaf walnut trees (*Juglans microcarpa*) create a uniquely vibrant combination of colors.

McKittrick Canyon is one of the most photographed canyons in the world, drawing people from not only the United States but also countries like Germany, Japan, England, Korea, China and Australia, just to name a few. The first annual fall color cavalcade was held in October 1971. (In the early days, McKittrick Canyon could be accessed only via guided tours led by park rangers.) This first tour was broken down into three groups totaling 135 people who enjoyed the unique experience. By 1979, the number of tour participants had increased to 2,800. Today, the color tours are self-

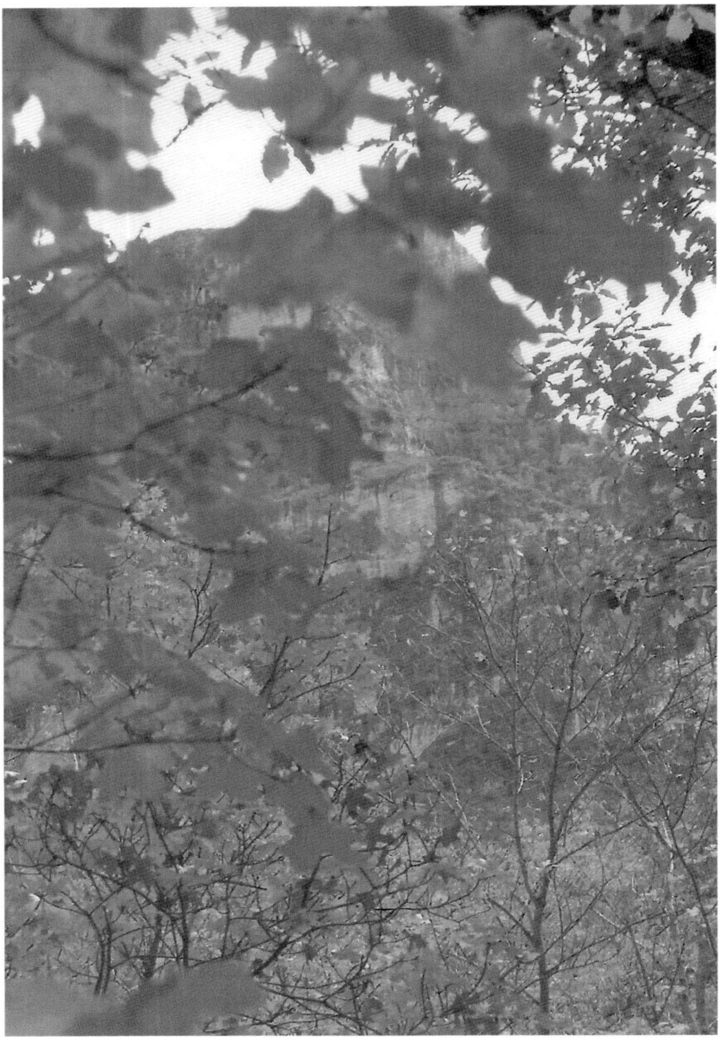

Bigtooth maples, normally found in northern regions, put on a big show in the fall. *Author's collection.*

guided, with park rangers scattered throughout the canyon to answer questions and make sure hikers are staying on the trails. There are 110 car slots in the parking lot, and these fill to capacity during the colorful weekends. The entrance road to the canyon has been known to have long lines of visitors waiting to be allowed into the lot as other vehicles filled with hikers leave.

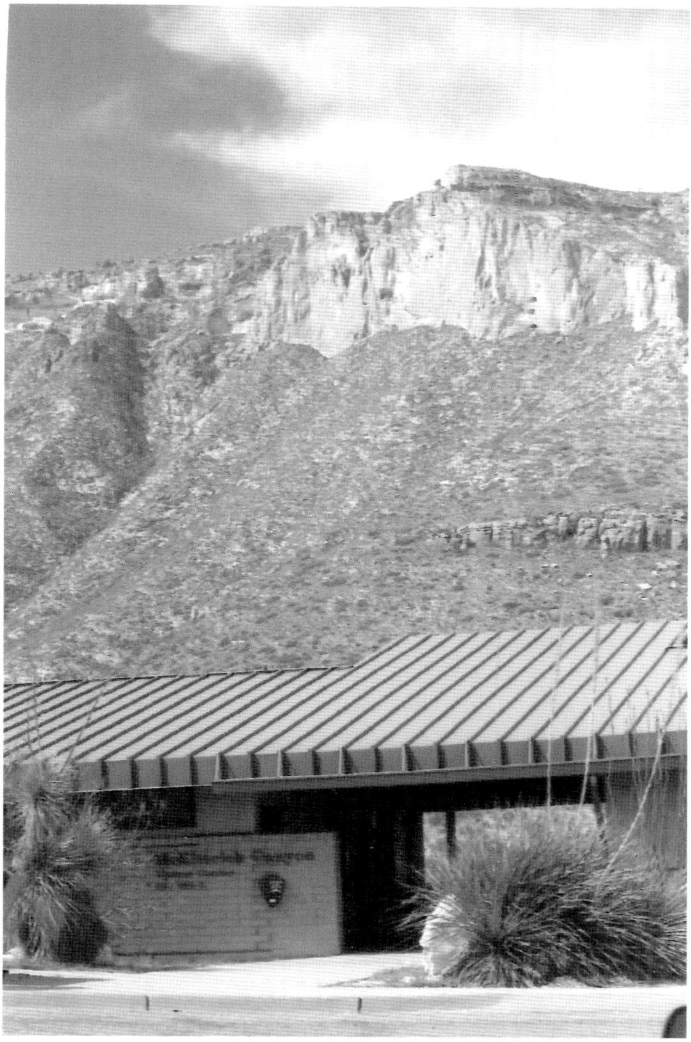

At the McKittrick Canyon Visitors' Center, visitors are treated to many informative and historical displays, as well as a short film hosted by Wallace Pratt. *Author's collection.*

When you first drive into the parking lot at the visitors' center, you might feel, as early settler Wallace Pratt felt, that the canyon appears to be nothing more than an arid desert setting. However, be prepared to be amazed by the continually changing landscape as you start the first leg of your journey.

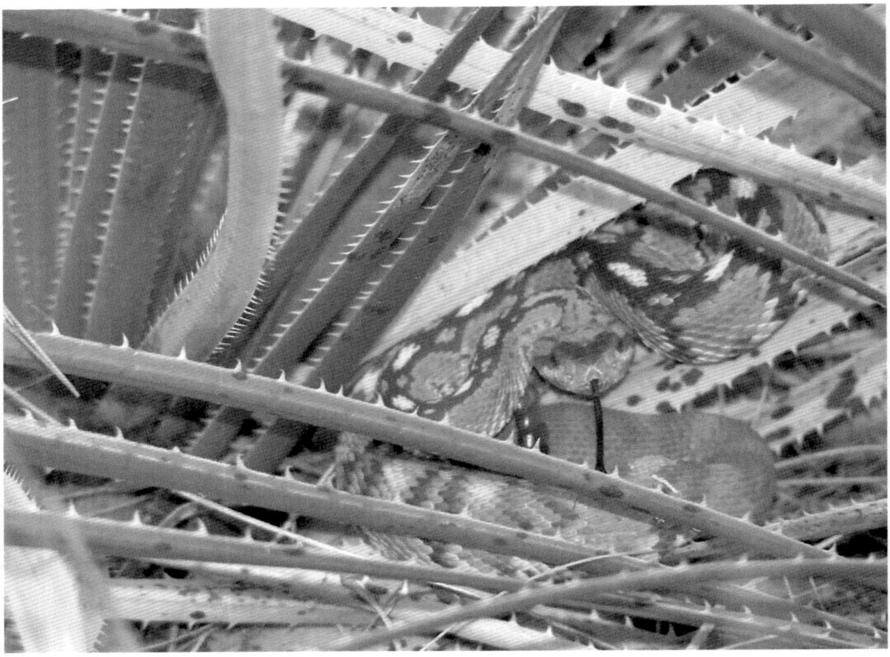

Although not seen very often, visitors should keep a keen eye out for rattlesnakes, as they blend in with the surrounding foliage and can surprise hikers. *Author's collection.*

At the beginning, the high desert setting presents rock ledges; deep, dry creek beds; and cacti. But soon juniper and piñon trees pop up, giving a hint of what is in store farther into the canyon. Your progression will take you deeper into a primal forest of ponderosa pine and Douglas fir surrounded by scatterings of several varieties of yucca and prickly pear. It is an odd combination that might seem out of place at first, but once you understand the complete diversity of the canyon, it will all make perfect sense. It is also in this area that you might find a mottled rattlesnake resting, so keep a watchful eye as you pass. Collared lizards aren't as common, but a keen eye can spot one sunning on a stone.

McKittrick Canyon is the only area in the Guadalupe Mountains in which the faxon yucca (*Yucca faxoniana*), also known as the Spanish dagger, will grow. In other parts of South Texas, the faxon yucca can grow to heights of over forty feet, but in McKittrick, the plant reaches only eighteen feet. Petals from the yucca are edible and can be used in salads or steamed; they have the waxy consistency of a leek and a slightly sweet taste. Often mistaken for a cactus, the yucca, which is the state flower of New Mexico, is actually in the lily family, as is the sotol. The yucca

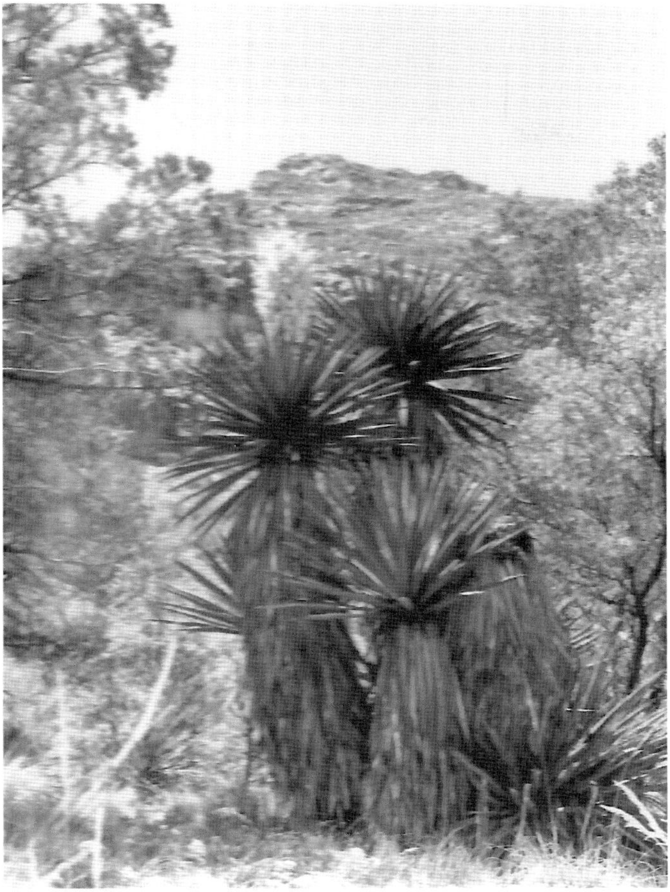

The stately faxon yucca, or Spanish dagger, can grow to over forty feet tall. It is the tallest of the Texas yuccas. *Courtesy Guadalupe Mountains National Park.*

provided the native tribes with many medicinal products, as well as soap, which was made from the roots.

The star of the show in the canyon has to be the Texas madrone, known not only for its striking beauty but also its extreme rarity. To protect the young saplings from marauding deer and goats, the park service encloses them in wire cages. It is an ongoing struggle to germinate and raise the madrone trees, as the species has a tendency of being touchy. The Texas madrone will produce small, white, lantern-shaped flowers in spring that will mature into small red berries in the fall. Studies have shown that the trees that grow in

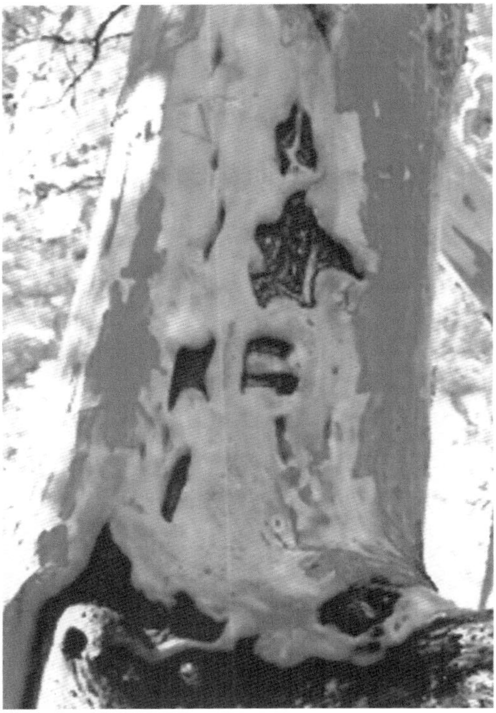

The smooth bark of the Texas madrone has garnered the tree several interesting names, including Lady's Leg. *Author's collection.*

the higher elevations produce berries of a deeper red. In the early days, these berries were gathered up and made into a tasty, sweet preserve. Generally, natives tried to find the trees with the least amount of berries remaining, as it was thought that these had a sweeter taste. The bitter berries were left for the raccoons and ringtails.

The leaves and bark of the madrone, both high in tannin, were used by the native tribes as a natural astringent, dye and diuretic. Called *manzanitas* (little apples) by the locals, madrones are evergreen trees with a unique feature—exfoliating bark. New bark can range in color from white to a deep red. Due to its smooth, red bark, the madrone tree goes by many names, some of which are provocative, including "Naked Indian" and "Lady's Leg." But in some parts of Texas, they are known as the strawberry tree, given that the berries resemble tiny strawberries. Most madrones reach to over forty feet tall and grow in the marginal habitat on the lower edge of the juniper forests but remain unproductive.

McKittrick Canyon's highest forests, part of the old boreal community, date back to the Pleistocene period and consist of ponderosa pine (*Pinus ponderosa*) and Douglas fir (*Pseudotsuga menziesii*). Since these forests have never been timbered, they are dense and lush.

McKittrick Creek chases alongside you. Although it's sometimes hidden, you can usually hear the gurgling of the brook. Being the only perennial stream in the park, this is extremely rare for such an arid region. Along the creek you can find wild strawberries and grapes flourishing in the moist soils.

CHAPTER 9
HISTORIC STRUCTURES OF MCKITTRICK CANYON

Humans have put their touch on McKittrick Canyon, from the midden rings of the rounded teepees used by the native tribes to evidence of the first white settlers.

Felix McKittrick's Dugout

Remnants of Felix McKittrick's crudely hewn dugout close to the mouth of his canyon can still be seen today. Located in the southwest quadrant of the southeast quadrant of Section 2, Block 65 in Township 1 of Culberson County, Texas, the crude dugout consisted of earthen walls on three sides and a front wall of broken Lamar limestone or flagstone facing the stream, which was approximately sixty-one feet away.

The walls were supported by a Y-shaped frame post at the entrance, and the roof consisted of wood and earth. This eight- by twelve-foot hole-in-the-wall (literally) is considered to be the oldest historic structure in the park. Located on the right side of the winding trail leading into McKittrick Canyon, the dugout, which is also situated on a slight ledge above the trail, is extremely difficult to locate due to the vegetation surrounding the dilapidated remnants.

Teacher, author and poet Robert Burlingame lived in the shadow of El Capitan after his retirement, and that is where he derived his inspiration for his last book, a tribute to his beloved landscape. With a cup of coffee in hand, Burlington would watch the sunrise from his study window as he sat in front of his manual typewriter. Inspiration would come from what he witnessed or thought about during the day. In this book, Burlingame wrote an ode to Felix McKittrick's dugout, a part of which follows:

Walking Past the Dugout of Felix McKittrick

Halfway up
or halfway down in this sparkling canyon
I see the dugout you gouged after the Civil War

rude hollow beneath the mountain
grown over with gray oak,
sotol and juniper

—these days a new trail
misses your doorway
by a half a hundred feet—

in that leafy place
the Apaches forgave you under
the limestone cliffs—somewhere, nowhere—
lit by moons as immense as sins.

Hunter's Lodge

Deep in McKittrick Canyon is an unassuming flagstone structure that, while rustic in its beauty, is not what one might expect of a millionaire oilman. Built in 1927 by J.C. Hunter Sr. and his partner, Matt Grisham, the stone structure known as Hunter's Lodge, which once served as a line camp for Hunter Sr., has changed little over the years.

Inside, wide, rough-hewn planks that were heavily chinked to fill in the knotholes covered the walls. A long porch invited visitors to sit back and relax while they took in the views of the surrounding peaks. Ever a conservationist, Hunter built the lodge around the trees instead of cutting them down. For many years, a tree grew out of the porch and living room;

however, the park service deemed this a hazard to the public and the structure, and it was cut down. The lodge was described as having very modest furnishings and curtains acquired from thrift stores and five-and-dime stores, but the heaters worked, there was always hot water and the iron beds were comfortable. Stories of wild desert lightning storms causing some frightening moments for Hunter's guests, who were sure they were going to be electrocuted as they slept in the metal beds, made great fodder for newspaper articles.

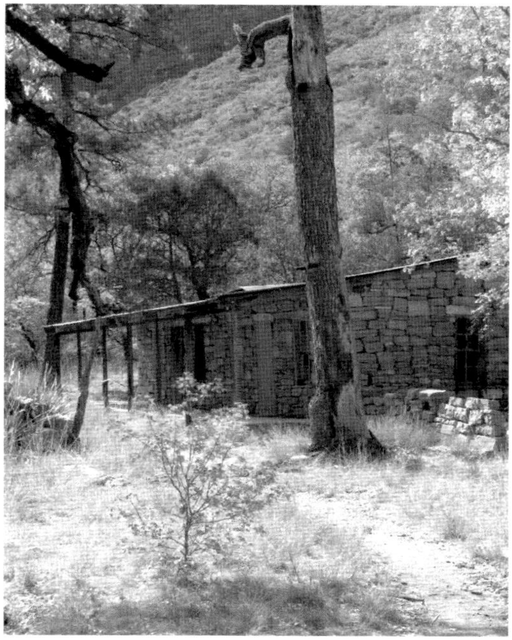

Hunter's Lodge is built out of slate and limestone supported by heart pine timbers. A pine tree once grew out of the roof of the front porch. *Author's collection.*

Stone Cabin

After his purchase of the land that included McKittrick Canyon, geologist Wallace Pratt decided to build a retirement home in the canyon for him and his first wife, Pearl Stuckey. Unfortunately, Pearl would not survive to see the completion of the structure. This home was to be known as the Stone Cabin, since Mr. Pratt despised the word "lodge" and the hunting connotations that accompany it. (Pratt never hunted or allowed anyone else to hunt on his land in McKittrick.) The cabin was to be built at the intersection between North and South McKittrick Canyon. Being in such a remote location, local stone was quarried close to McKittrick Canyon. From this stone was built a unique cabin consisting of a bedroom, a bathroom, a living/dining room and a functional kitchen. The cabin was to be a respite for the Pratt family from the hot, humid weather of Houston, Texas.

Designed to be constructed solely of stone and wood, the Stone Cabin featured heart pine rafters, collar beams and sheathing that supported the heavy slate roof, which was shipped to McKittrick Canyon from East Texas. Pratt enlisted the help of several amazing people to build the cabin, including a stonemason from Sweetwater, Texas; a civil engineer; two local ranch hands; and two cowboys with their horses. The stone walls were raised by the cowboys, who looped lassos around their saddle horns and had their horses drag the heavy stones up a plank to the top of the walls. A two-car garage located behind the Stone Cabin was constructed in the same manner.

Holding true to the stone theme, a large slab of limestone described as a perfect natural hexagon—twelve feet long by five feet wide and three inches thick—was installed on four-foot legs to create a picnic table that is still used today. At the insistence of Pratt's second wife, Mrs. Iris Calderhead Pratt, each window of the Stone Cabin was aligned so that a view of a beautiful peak could be enjoyed. One of these views is of a stone cliff known as Lover's Leap—the origin of this name is unknown, but it is one of the most spectacular rock faces in the canyon.

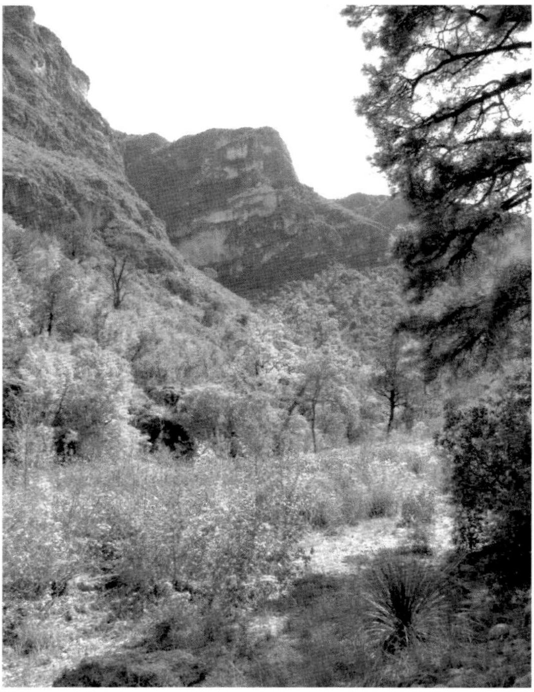

This imposing mountain is called Lover's Leap, although there are no records of any tragic events occurring to warrant the name. *Author's collection.*

Pratt himself selected "silty limestone, thin-bedded and closely jointed by clean vertical features." Workers scraped off the thin layers of earth to reveal the proper stones, and the stonemasons used crowbars as levers to pry the stones apart. Pratt was proud to say that very few of the stones required the use of hammer and chisel to fit.

Through the plans of architect John F. Staub, the walls, fireplace, floors and, most uniquely, roof were all stone. This not only provided a secure home for the Pratts but also protected the structure, should a fire ever threaten the canyon. The Stone Cabin was intended to be a retirement home after its completion in 1930. This plan took a different turn when the Pratts were trapped in the cabin during a large, frightening flash flood that left the family stranded for nearly a week. Mrs. Pratt was not eager to go back after this experience and no longer wanted it to be their permanent residence.

The Stone Cabin furnishings were sparse but comfortable, featuring two reclining Adirondack chairs, four beds and assorted hammocks, which provided room for guests inside and on the porch of the structure. The crowning glory of the cabin was a special handmade dining table and chairs that sat twelve. The massive refectory table, four feet wide by eighteen feet long, had many a dignitary seated around it over the years. This table set, made by Mexican artisans out of ebony, or ironwood, was a gift from a Pratt family friend, Edgar Tobin, of San Antonio, Texas, and was later moved to the Carlsbad Public Library in Carlsbad, New Mexico, where it served as a conference table for many years. It was during the table's time at the public library that it was vandalized by local youths. The library paid to have the table completely restored and covered with a substantial piece of glass to further protect the artifact. Eventually, the National Park Service wanted to restore the table to its proper setting and considered moving it to the Stone Cabin. Transporting such a large, heavy table to the remote spot posed a problem. After much discussion and fielding many ideas ranging from horses to helicopters, it was decided that the table would be better suited to adorn the Pratts' more recent home, the Ship on the Desert.

Unfortunately, after the Pratts moved into their new home, the Stone Cabin fell into disrepair and was under threat of destruction. A restoration project in the 1970s saved the cabin. In 1985, an infestation of wood-boring ants threatened the cabin once again, but the park service was able to control the pests and continues to monitor the structure for any other threats. When the necessity of the repair of the roof of the Stone Cabin arose, each stone was individually removed, numbered and then replaced exactly where it had once been in the original design.

Today, the Stone Cabin is a favorite destination along the rocky trail in McKittrick, providing hikers with a place to sit down, relax under a huge Texas madrone and imagine what it must have been like to have the privilege to call this little piece of heaven home. The National Register of Historic Buildings lists the cabin and its outbuildings, which also have slate roofs, as a historic landmark.

Ship on the Desert

Since his wife had been rattled by the flood, Wallace Pratt changed his retirement plan by building a new home on his land to the south of McKittrick Canyon. This home was called the Ship on the Desert to reassure his wife that they would be safe. People would often make the mistake of calling the home the "Ship of the Desert," to which Pratt would reply, "A ship of the desert is a camel."

Being an oilman, Pratt designed the Ship on the Desert to look like an oil tanker. Styled much like Frank Lloyd Wright–designed homes with clean lines and open vistas, it was built to mirror Pratt's career with the oil industry. This home is also listed in the National Register. Currently, the home is used to house traveling members of the park service, as well as researchers.

Construction on the Pratts' new home began in 1941 but was delayed by World War II. This did not deter Long Island, New York architect Newton Bevin, however, who lived at the Stone Cabin with his wife, Elizabeth, during the actual construction of the new house by contractor Ed Birdsell of Carlsbad, New Mexico. The narrow, rectangular structure measured

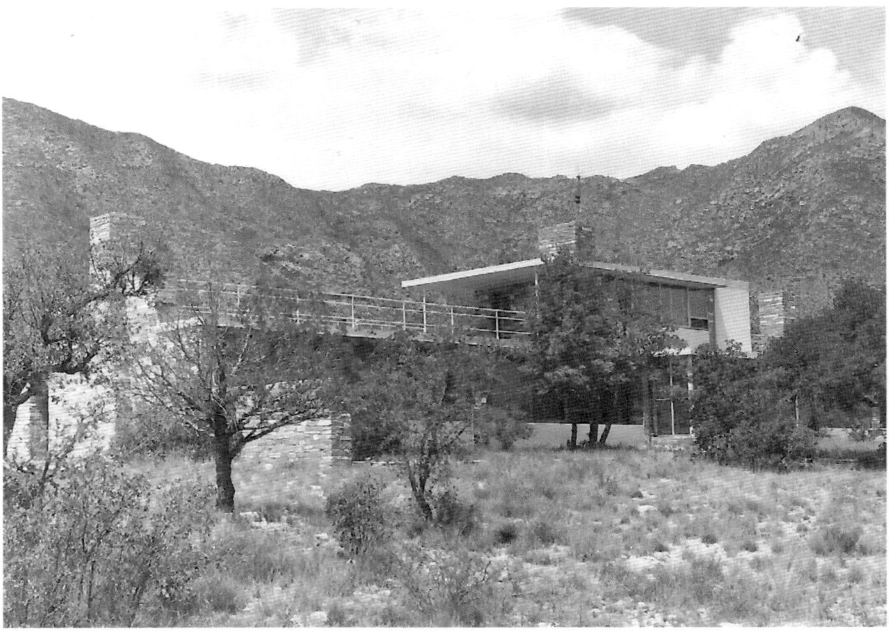

Built in the style of famed architect Frank Lloyd Wright, the Ship on the Desert gave a unique element to McKittrick Canyon. *Courtesy Guadalupe Mountains National Park.*

only 16 feet wide by 110 feet long and was made of stone, steel and windows in the International style, complete with spiral staircase. From the large windows, spectacular views of the surrounding Guadalupe Mountains can be seen. Seven massive transverse stone walls tied together with steel trusses make up the skeleton of the Ship on the Desert. The second-story amidships is glass, from which you can see as far as the Davis Mountains to the southeast. Pratt noted, "The architect literally put each stone in place, so distributing the various shades of soft gray and brown rock tints as to yield a pleasing harmony."

Pratt and his third wife, Suzanne d'Autremont, had primarily lived in a New York City apartment before his retirement. One of the prized possessions from that home was his set of massive maple bookshelves, which he brought with him to the Ship on the Desert. They are still featured proudly in the home.

The home also featured a two-car garage that housed his and hers matching Mercedes Benzes. A spare guest room was attached to the garage, and there was also a greenhouse, stables, an electric power plant and a landing strip. Due to the isolated location, the home did not have electricity or telephone service. The electricity was generated in the electric plant by a large diesel engine, and Pratt had a radio receiver for emergencies, on which he was always proud to announce that the only reception he received was from the Canadian Broadcasting Agency out of Ottawa, Canada.

The Ship on the Desert is situated away from McKittrick Canyon proper, so the park service uses the structure for educational purposes, and it is possible for researchers to rent the home for a nominal daily fee. Dormitory accommodations are available, and the space must be shared with other researchers. The home is maintained by the park service, which has replaced the roof several times over the years.

Pratt was to build a third home on his remaining acreage near his beloved McKittrick Canyon—this one on the same road as the Ship on the Desert but closer to the national park access route.

Another obscure structure in McKittrick Canyon is a small house built in 1928 on a ledge above the Grisham-Hunter Lodge. The home was constructed by Willis Smith and Jesse Parrish, employees of J.C. Hunter Sr. Allegedly the pair was promised $600 for their time and labor upon the completion of this structure, but when Hunter refused to pay for whatever reason, Parrish moved off to Van Horn, Texas, where he died.

No matter the history, each of these structures left its mark on the landscape of McKittrick Canyon for future generations to study and enjoy.

CHAPTER 10
THE FUTURE OF MCKITTRICK CANYON

In 2013, McKittrick Canyon, as well as much of the Guadalupe Mountains National Park, experienced a devastating flood that closed the canyon for a few months as rangers struggled to clear trails of debris. The path of destruction changed the flow of the canyon from the familiar walkways used by so many in the past to newly constructed trails in the approximate locations. The canyon has seen many changes during its existence, and this will certainly be chalked up to a time when McKittrick reinvented itself yet again.

According to Congress, the purpose of a national park is "to conserve the scenery and the natural and historic objects and the wildlife therein and to provide for the enjoyment of the same in such manner and by such means as will leave them unimpaired for the enjoyment of future generations."

When President Lyndon B. Johnson signed the Wilderness Act (which celebrated its fiftieth anniversary in 2014) into existence on September 3, 1964, he was quoted as saying, "If future generations are to remember us with gratitude rather than contempt, we must leave them a glimpse of the world as it was in the beginning, not just after we got through with it." The signing was the culmination of sixty drafts and eight long years of work on the project. In its text, the Wilderness Act defines a wilderness thusly: "A wilderness, in contrast with those areas where man and his own works dominate the landscape, is hereby recognized as an area where the earth and its community of life are untrammeled by man, where man himself is a visitor who does not remain."

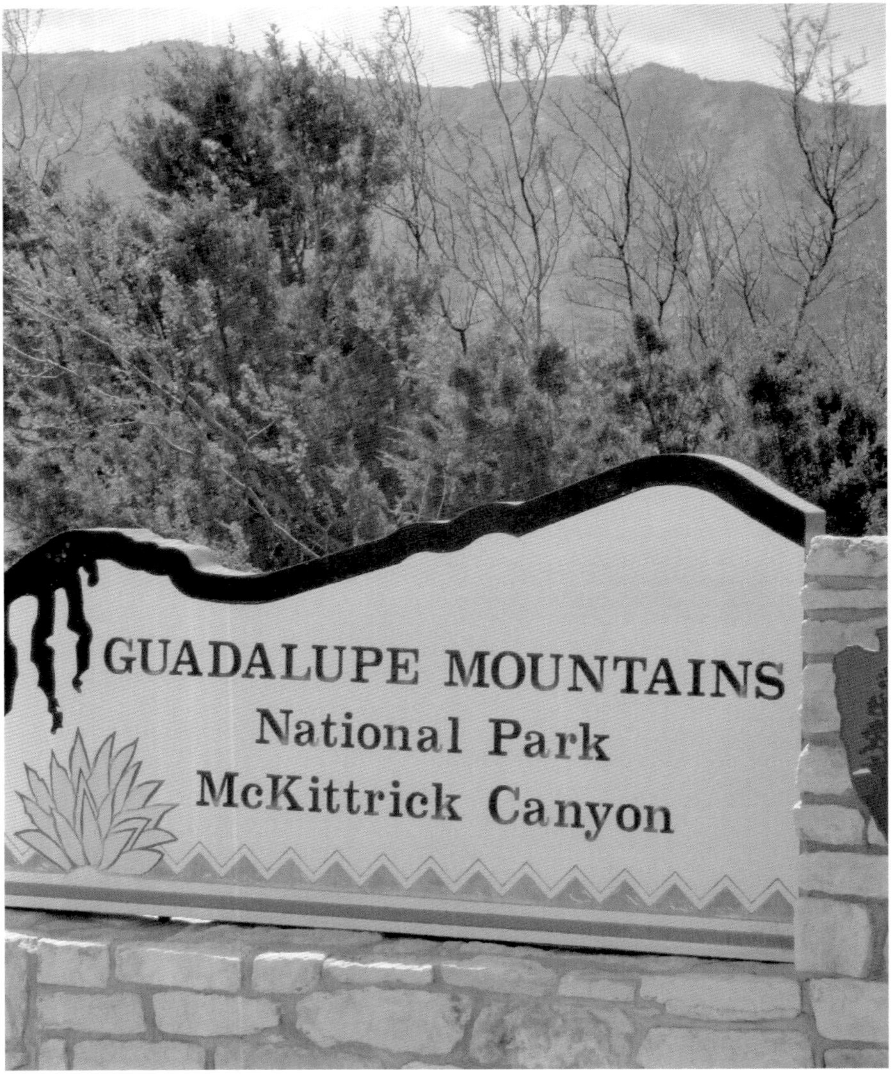

The McKittrick Canyon sign located just off the highway is the first introduction visitors get to the beauty of the canyon. *Author's collection.*

As with any piece of legislature, the Wilderness Act is not without its critics. Criteria to determine what a wilderness truly is are oftentimes vague and up to loose interpretation, which creates heated debate on both sides of the coin. Congressional bills are being introduced constantly for consideration to create new wilderness areas across the United States.

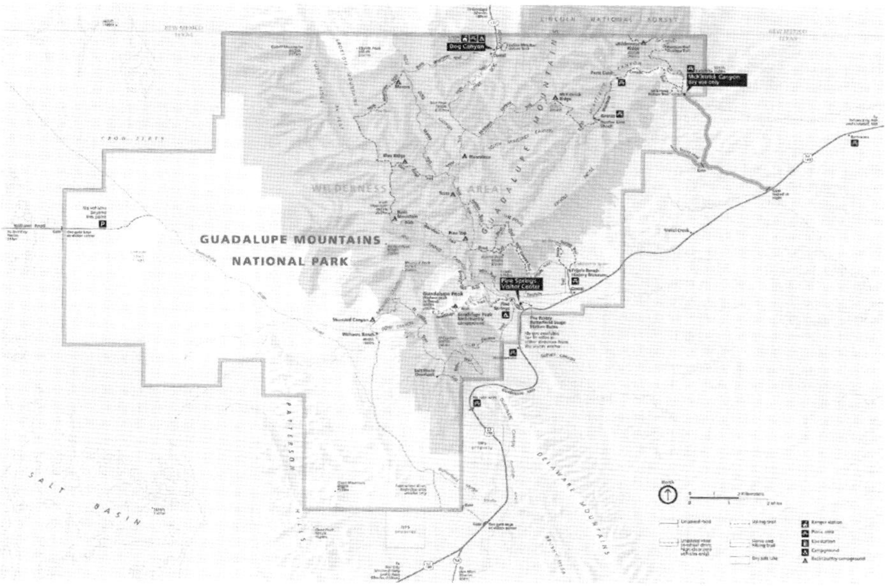

This map shows the vastness of the Guadalupe Mountains National Park system. *National Park Service.*

It is the intention of the National Park Service to keep the Guadalupe Mountains "wild." According to the National Park Service brochure *Keeping It Wild: The Guadalupe Mountains Wilderness*, "Wilderness areas offer glimpses into the past and provide places to envision the future."

Oil production is in full swing, which concerns the National Park Service. Although oil drilling will never be allowed in the park, it is happening in the surrounding countryside, and the NPS believes this could have a negative impact on the park in the future.

All in all, McKittrick Canyon is relatively young to the national parks system, with the visitors' center being completed in 1982, even though the massive limestone reef walls that rise two thousand feet behind the center are 260 to 270 million years old.

Park crews and volunteers are working on removing inactive power lines from McKittrick Canyon. When this is complete, the canyon will have a fresh, open concept for visitors to enjoy.

Today's visitors will make the biggest impact on those of tomorrow. Please be respectful of the park and all that it entails. The National Park Service hopes that McKittrick Canyon remains a go-to destination for serious and recreational hikers and researchers alike, and it is the organization's full intention to preserve the unique beauty that is McKittrick Canyon in the pristine manner in which it exists today. According to park records, 10 to 15 percent of park visitors come from foreign countries, while 40 percent come from the state of Texas and the rest hail from other parts of the United States.

According to Dr. Jonena Hearst, geologist for the Guadalupe Mountains National Park, McKittrick Canyon will remain the same, geologically speaking, but "scientists will continue to refine our understanding of the Middle Permian and McKittrick Canyon will continue to play a role in that in large part because it is so accessible for study."

Probably the best description of McKittrick Canyon comes from the National Park Service website:

> *While the towering walls of McKittrick Canyon protect the riches of diversity, its precious secrets are hidden in riparian oasis. It is no wonder that it has been described as the "most beautiful spot in Texas." But for all its magical power that delights thousands of people each year, its fragility reminds us that our enjoyment cannot compromise its necessity for survival. It must survive—not for us, but for all that lives within. Thousands of visitors come to Guadalupe Mountains National Park to visit McKittrick Canyon each year, especially during the latter part of October or early November for the sensational fall colors. In this tiny part of West Texas, the foliage (brilliant reds, subtle yellows and deep browns) contrasts dramatically with the flavor of the arid Chihuahuan Desert that includes century plants, prickly pear cacti, black-tail rattlers, steep canyon walls and crystal clear blue skies. Whether you come for the fall show or plan your trip for another season, the beauty of McKittrick Canyon is always breathtaking.*

BIBLIOGRAPHY

Books and Brochures

Adams, Clarence S., and Joan N. Adams. *Riders of the Pecos and the Seven Rivers Outlaws*. Roswell, NM: Old-Time Publications, 1990.

Adams, Clarence S., and Tom E. Brown. *Three Ranches West: A True Story of John S. Chisum, the Cowman Who Opened the West for the Cattle Trade*. New York: Carlton Press, 1972.

Allender, Michael, and Alan Tenant. *The Guadalupe Mountains of Texas*. Austin: University of Texas Press, 1984.

Balgemann, William H. *New Mexico's Guadalupe Mountain Area, 1535–1977: A Brief Historical Resume of the Area*. Carlsbad, NM: self-published, 1979.

Ball, Eve. *In the Days of Victorio: Recollections of a Warm Springs Apache*. Tucson: University of Arizona Press, 1972.

Ball, Eve, Nora Henn and Lynda Sánchez. *Indéh: An Apache Odyssey*. Provo, UT: Brigham Young University Press, 1980.

Basehart, Harry W. *Mescalero Apache Subsistence Patterns and Sociopolitical Organization*. New York: Garland Press, 1974.

Buchanan, Kimberly Moore. *Apache Women Warriors*. Austin: University of Texas Press, 2000.

Caldwell, Clifford R. *John S. Chisum: Cattle King of the Pecos Revisited*. Santa Fe, NM: Sunstone Press, 2010.

Castetter, Edward F., and Morris E. Opler. *The Ethnobotany of the Chiricahua and Mescalero Apache*. Albuquerque: University of New Mexico Press, 1936.

Clarke, Mary Whatley. *John Simpson Chisum: Jingle-Bob King of the Pecos*. Austin, TX: Eakin Press, 1984.

Convis, Charles L. *Outlaw Tales of Texas: True Stories of the Lone Star State's Most Infamous Crooks, Culprits, and Cutthroats*. Guilford, CT: Two Dot, 2012.

Cremony, John C. *Life Among the Apaches*. Lincoln: University of Nebraska Press, 1983.

Dobie, J. Frank. *Coronado's Children*. Austin: University of Texas Press, 1982.

———. *Legends of Texas*. Dallas, TX: Southern Methodist University Press, 1924.

———. *Rattlesnakes*. Austin: University of Texas Press, 1965.

Douglas, C.L. *Cattle Kings of Texas*. Buffalo Gap, TX: State House Press, 1989.

Douglas, William O. *Farewell to Texas: A Vanishing Wilderness*. New York: McGraw-Hill, 1967.

Fabry, Judith K. *Guadalupe Mountains National Park: An Administrative History*. Santa Fe, NM: Division of History, Southwest Cultural Resource Center, Southwest Region, National Parks Service, Department of the Interior, 1990.

Foreman, Grant. *Marcy and the Gold Seekers*. Norman: University of Oklahoma Press, 1939.

Genoways, Hugh H., and Robert J. Baker, eds. *Biological Investigations in the Guadalupe Mountains National Park, Texas: Proceedings of a Symposium Held at Texas Tech University, Lubbock, Texas—April 4–5, 1975*. Washington, D.C.: National Park Service, 1979.

Girard, Roselle M. *Texas Rocks and Minerals*. Austin: University of Texas Press, 1964.

Greenberg, Adolph M. *Ethnographic Overview and Assessment of Guadalupe Mountains National Park*. N.p., 1986.

Greene, A.C. *900 Miles on the Butterfield Trail*. Denton: University of North Texas Press, 2006.

Haley, James L. *Apaches: A History and Culture Portrait*. Norman: University of Oklahoma Press, 1997.

Hand, George O. *The Civil War in Apacheland: Sergeant George Hand's Diary: California, Arizona, West Texas, New Mexico, 1861–1864*. Silver City, NM: High Lonesome Books, 1996.

Hunter, John M. *The Trail Drivers of Texas*. Nashville, TN: Cokesbury Press, 1925.

Jameson, W.C. *Buried Treasures of the American Southwest*. Atlanta, GA: August House Publishers, 2006.

———. *Buried Treasures of Texas*. Atlanta, GA: August House Publishers, 2006.

———. *The Guadalupe Mountains: Island in the Desert*. El Paso: Texas Western Press, 1994.

———. *Legends and Lore of the Guadalupe Mountains*. Albuquerque: University of New Mexico Press, 2007.

———. *Lost Mines and Buried Treasures of the Guadalupe Mountains*. N.p.: CreateSpace Independent Publishing, 2011.

Julyan, Robert. *The Mountains of New Mexico*. Albuquerque: University of New Mexico Press, 2006.

Klasner, Lily. *My Girlhood Among Outlaws*. Edited by Eve Ball. Tucson: University of Arizona Press, 1972.

Kurtz, Don. *Trails of the Guadalupes: A Hiker's Guide to the Trails of the Guadalupe Mountains National Park*. Champaign, IL: Environmental Associates, 1982.

Levy, Benjamin. *Guadalupe Mountains National Park: Historic Resource Study*. Washington, D.C.: Department of the Interior, Division of History, Office of Archeology and Historic Preservation, 1971.

Ligon, J. Stokely. *New Mexico Birds and Where to Find Them*. Albuquerque: University of New Mexico Press, 1971.

Massey, Sara R., ed. *Black Cowboys of Texas*. College Station: Texas A&M University Press, 2004.

McKittrick, Fred L. *The McKitricks and Roots of Ulster Scots*. Baltimore, MD: Gateway Press, 1979.

Moody, Ralph. *Geronimo: Wolf of the Warpath*. New York: Sterling Publishing Company, 2006.

Murphy, Dan. *The Guadalupes: Guadalupe Mountains National Park*. Carlsbad, NM: Carlsbad Caverns Natural History Association, 1984.

National Park Service. *Guadalupe Mountains: The Permian Reef Trail Guide*. Washington, D.C.: National Park Service, n.d.

———. *Guadalupe Mountains: Roadside Geology Guide*. Washington, D.C.: National Park Service, n.d.

Nolan, Frederick. *The Lincoln County War: A Documentary History*. Norman: University of Oklahoma Press, 1992.

Obert, Donald D. *Narrative Report on McKittrick Canyon, Culberson County, Texas*. Prepared for the Texas State Park Board, Austin, TX, 1938.

Olin, George. *Mammals of the Southwest Deserts*. Globe, AZ: Southwest Parks and Monuments Association, 1954.

Opler, Morris E. *Apache Odyssey*. New York: Holt, Rinehart and Winston, 1969.

Parent, Laurence, and Joe Nick Patoski. *Texas Mountains*. Austin: University of Texas Press, 2001.

Penfield, Thomas. *Dig Here!: Lost Mines and Buried Treasures of the Southwest*. Kempton, IL: Adventures Unlimited Press, 2004.

———. *Guide to Treasure in Texas*. Carson City, NV: Carson Enterprises, 1972.

Perry, Richard John. *Western Apache Heritage: People of the Mountain Corridor.* Austin: University of Texas Press, 1991,

Phenix, Vince. *History of Wallace Pratt Lodge.* Guadalupe National Parks Service Library, Pine Springs, TX, 1981.

Poe, Sophie. *Buckboard Days.* Caldwell, ID: Caxton Printers, 1936.

Probert, Thomas. *Lost Mines and Buried Treasures of the West.* Berkeley: University of California Press, 1977.

Robinson, Sherry K. *Apache Voices: Their Stories of Survival as Told to Eve Ball.* Albuquerque: University of New Mexico Press, 2000.

Savoy, Carlos. *Texas Tales of Lost Mines and Buried Treasures.* Boulder, CO: Taylor Trade Publishing, 2001.

Schmidly, David J. *Mammals of Trans-Pecos Texas: Including Big Bend National Park and Guadalupe Mountains National Park.* College Station: Texas A&M University Press, 1977.

Schneider, Bill. *Hiking Carlsbad Caverns and Guadalupe Mountains National Parks.* Helena, MT: Falcon Press, 1996.

Sonnichsen, C.L. *Geronimo and the End of the Apache Wars.* Lincoln: University of Nebraska Press, 1990.

———. *The Mescalero Apaches.* Norman: University of Oklahoma Press, 1973.

Switzer, Ronald R. *Tobacco, Pipes and Cigarettes of the Pre-Historic Southwest.* El Paso, TX: El Paso Archaeological Society, 1969.

Tolbert, Robert X. *Tolbert of Texas: The Man and His Work.* Fort Worth: Texas Christian University Press, 1986.

Watson, Mrs. Ben. *Hidden Gold of the Guadalupes.* Schoenchen, KS: Tumbleweed Press, 1968.

Williams, Jack R. *Indians of the Guadalupes.* Carlsbad, NM: Carlsbad Caverns Natural History Association in cooperation with the National Park Service, 1956.

PERIODICALS

Anderson, Eugene. "Hidden Gold of the Guadalupes." *True Treasure* (November–December 1972): 28–31.

———. "Missing Cache of the James Brothers." *True Treasure* (May–June 1975): 12–16.

———. "Ruins of Massacred Wagon Train Discovered." *True Treasure* (September–October 1969).

———. "The Treasure Cave of Juniper Springs." *Western Treasures* (November 1969): 32–35.

Benz, Donald N. "Sword of Revenge." *Golden West* (September 1965): 28–31.

Carson, Xanthus. "Gold in the Guadalupes." *True Frontier* (Fall 1976): 6–10, 57–60.

Klepper, Don. "Treasure of the Guadalupes." *Texas Parks and Wildlife* 26 (n.d.): 24–27.

Lee, Ronald J. "Archeological Survey of McKittrick Canyon Entrance Road." *Self*, August 14, 1974.

Parent, Annette Richards. "Guadalupe: Barrier Reef in the Desert." *National Parks and Conservation Magazine* 48, no. 10 (October 1974): 4–9.

Smith, Ralph A. "'Long' Webster and the 'Vile Industry of Selling Scalps.'" *West Texas Historical Association Year Book* 37 (October 1961): 99–120.

VIDEO RECORDINGS

Bayside Media Services. *A History & Tour of the Guadalupe Mountains National Park*: Oakland, CA: Bayside Media Services, 2007.

INDEX

ABOUT THE AUTHOR

As a writer and photographer, Donna Blake Birchell greatly appreciates the beauty and gifts of nature. McKittrick Canyon has long been a part of Birchell's personal history and a favorite respite. She believes that this uniquely diverse canyon should have its own story told and not be just a short chapter or footnote in other works. It is her hope that this work will entice many others to travel and discover the wonders waiting for them in the unassuming high desert Texas canyon.

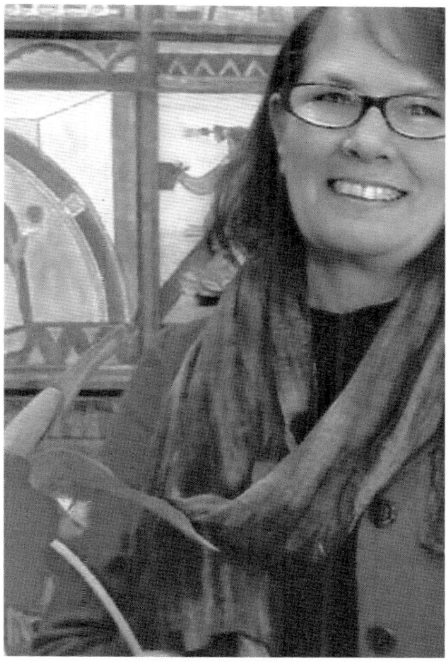